Christmas Gifts

from the **Kitchen**

D0795524

Photo Legend front and back cover:

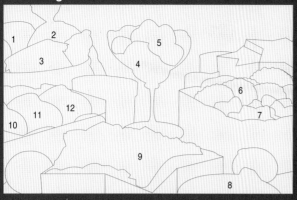

1. Fiesta Relish, page 85
2. Wheat And Walnut Crackers, page 110
3. Cilantro Sunflower Pesto, page 91
4. Hazelnut Truffles, page 138
5. Pink Chocolate Truffles, page 138
6. Jam Jams, page 16
7. Lemon Almond Snowflakes, page 24
8. Peppermint Patties, page 34
9. Cashew Buttercrunch, page 120
10. Special Curry Rub, page 54
11. Cajun Seasoning, page 54
12. Tomato Basil Seasoning, page 53

Christmas Gifts from the Kitchen
Copyright © Company's Coming Publishing Limited

All rights reserved worldwide. No part of this book may be reproduced, stored in a retrieval system or transmitted in any form by any means without written permission in advance from the publisher.

In the case of photocopying or other reprographic copying, a license may be purchased from the Canadian Copyright Licensing Agency (Access Copyright). Visit www.accesscopyright.ca or call toll free 1-800-893-5777. In the United States, please contact the Copyright Clearance Centre at www.copyright.com or call 978-646-8600.

Brief portions of this book may be reproduced for review purposes, provided credit is given to the source. Reviewers are invited to contact the publisher for additional information.

First Printing October 2005

Library and Archives Canada Cataloguing in Publication

Paré, Jean, 1927-
        Christmas gifts from the kitchen / Jean Paré.

(Special occasion series)
Includes index.
ISBN 1-896891-73-X

        1. Christmas cookery. 2. Gifts. 3. Handicraft.
I. Title. II. Series: Paré, Jean, 1927- Special occasion series.

TX739.2.C45P368 2005   641.5'686   C2005-900795-8

Published by
Company's Coming Publishing Limited
2311 – 96 Street
Edmonton, Alberta, Canada T6N 1G3
Tel: 780-450-6223   Fax: 780-450-1857
www.companyscoming.com

Company's Coming is a registered trademark owned by Company's Coming Publishing Limited

Printed in China

Pictured at Top Left and Bottom Left: Gouda Chive Crackers, page 107
Centre Right: Cheese Puffs, page 107

Christmas Gifts from the Kitchen was created
thanks to the dedicated efforts of the people and
organizations listed below.

Company's Coming Publishing Limited

Author	Jean Paré
President	Grant Lovig
VP Product Development	Derrick Sorochan
Design Director	Jaclyn Draker
Publishing Coordinator	Shelly Willsey
	Carlene Chrisp
Senior Designer	Zoë Henry

The Recipe Factory

Research & Development Manager	Nora Prokop
	Roxanne Higuchi
Editor	Audrey Carroll
Associate Editors	Kari Christie
	Joan McManners
Copywriters	Kari Christie
	Debbie Dixon
	Joan McManners
Proofreaders	Pam Phillips
	Connie Townsend
Senior Food Editor	Lynda Elsenheimer
Food Editor	Jessica Assaly
Recipe Editors	Mary Anne Korn
	Lovoni Walker
Kitchen Services Manager	Jill Corbett
Test Kitchen Staff	James Bullock
	Laurie Stempfle
	Gloria Clare
Photo Editor	Paula Bertamini
Photography	Stephe Tate Photo
Photographer's Assistant	Ron Checora
Food Stylist	Ashley Billey
Prep Kitchen Coordinator	Audrey Smetaniuk
Prep Assistant	Linda Dobos
Prop Stylist	Snez Ferenac
Registered Dietitian	Margaret Ng
Research And Development Assistant	Jackie Ayotte

We gratefully acknowledge the following suppliers for their
generous support of our Test Kitchen and Photo Studio:

Corelle®
Hamilton Beach®
Lagostina®
Proctor Silex® Canada
Tupperware®

Our special thanks to the following businesses for providing
extensive props for photography:

A Taste of Provence	Linens 'N Things
Anchor Hocking Canada	Michaels The Arts and Crafts Store
Bernardin Ltd.	Mikasa Home Store
Browne & Co.	Pfaltzgraff Canada
Canadian Tire	Pier 1 Imports
Canhome Global	Sears Canada
Casa Bugatti	Stokes
Cherison Enterprises Inc.	The Bay
Corelle®	The Paderno Factory Store
Danesco Inc.	Totally Bamboo
Dansk Gifts	Winners Stores
Klass Works	

Table of Contents

Foreword

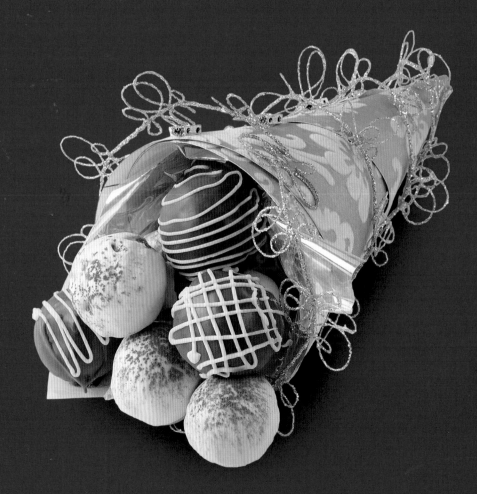

Christmas is such a precious time of year, filled with excited children, sparkling trees, festive music and family feasts. It's also the season of giving, a chance for us to convey our love to others with a special gesture of goodwill. Homemade gifts—personal expressions of affection and friendship—are always my favourite to give and to receive. I think many of us feel this way, which is why we've created *Christmas Gifts from the Kitchen*.

A gift from the kitchen, especially one carefully chosen to fit the occasion, makes a statement. It says, "I'm never too busy to create something just for you, because you're special to me." In these days when so many of us struggle to find some spare time in our busy lives, this message is especially meaningful.

Christmas Gifts from the Kitchen offers a wide selection of traditional and innovative gift ideas that are easy to make, along with plenty of creative and fun ways to decorate and wrap them up. This is a great opportunity to invite your family into the kitchen to help you with the seasonal preparations. And the best part of these gifts is that many of them can be made well ahead of the Christmas season rush.

The recipes in this book make it simple to find the perfect gift for everyone on your list. If you're looking for something fun to give to grandchildren, nieces or nephews, check out the Candy Christmas Tree and Sugar Cube Igloo projects in *Kits for Kids*, and be sure to join in the family fun by lending a helping hand in the assembly. Is the neighbour always helping you shovel your walk? Show your appreciation with a ready-to-make mix of spiced tea, hot chocolate or soup from *Dry Mixes*. And for the aunt who has everything, make an elegant gift of truffles from *Sweet Treats* and just watch her reaction. In addition to all the delightfully tempting and festive recipes, there are also some unique *Gifts for the Home*—relaxing bath bags, aromatic potpourri and even pet treats.

If lack of time is a challenge for you this holiday season, let me offer a few suggestions. Most cookies, squares and fudge recipes can be made and frozen as early as November. Christmas cake and pudding actually need the extra time to ripen. You can even start making some of the preserved recipes from *Gifts in a Jar* in late summer or early fall. In the chapter introductions, we've included advice on the best ways to freeze and store your homemade gifts well ahead of the holiday rush. Just imagine...you could have many of your gifts ready before December has even arrived!

Ideas to wrap your kitchen creations are pictured throughout the book. We've also offered a few interesting craft projects to get you started. The directions are clear and easy to follow, guiding you from start to finish. The chapter on *Wrapping It Up* is especially dedicated to unique gift bags and bows, handcrafted gift tags, and themed gift baskets. Using our ideas and your imagination, you can wrap up your gifts in your own unique style.

There are so many caring people who touch our lives throughout the year and Christmas is when we have the chance to say, "Thank you," "I love you," "You're in our thoughts," "We wish you well," or to give them a gift... just because. A gift from the kitchen—carefully chosen, meticulously prepared and lovingly decorated—takes these messages and wraps them up beautifully.

Long after the family parties and friendly gatherings have faded into memories of goodwill and generosity, this gracious message will continue to hold fast throughout the year. And that really is the best gift of all!

Merry Christmas everyone, and enjoy the season!

Jean Paré

Each recipe has been analyzed using the most up-to-date version of the Canadian Nutrient File from Health Canada, which is based on the United States Department of Agriculture (USDA) Nutrient Data Base. If more than one ingredient is listed (such as "hard margarine or butter"), or a range is given (1 – 2 tsp., 5 – 10 mL), then the first ingredient or amount is used in the analysis. Where an ingredient reads "sprinkle," "optional," or "for garnish," it is not included as part of the nutrition information. Milk, unless stated otherwise, is 1% and cooking oil, unless stated otherwise, is canola.

Margaret Ng, B.Sc. (Hon), M.A.
Registered Dietitian

Getting Ready

Gift Giving Made Easy

Plan ahead! Decide what homemade creations to prepare for those on your Christmas list. Make non-perishable gifts and preserves early in the fall. Start baking 1 to 2 months before Christmas and stock your freezer and pantry. With all the available goodies at hand, it will be easy to put gift baskets together in December.

Avoid giving scented gifts to someone with a sensitive nose or sweets to someone watching their weight. Keeping personal interests, hobbies or decor in mind means your homemade gifts will always be well-received. Keep a list of everyone you plan to give to, noting special interests or allergies so you won't forget.

Consider quantity when making your gifts. Don't give a couple something that serves ten, or a small box of candy to a family of six.

Your florist and even your own backyard are great resources for inexpensive package decorations. Plant flowers in your garden in the spring that can be dried in the fall for adorning packages at Christmastime. Tie a sprig of holly or a piece of cedar bough to the outside of a present or glue some pinecones to a gift jar.

Include children and other family members in your Christmas preparations. They can tie bows, make package decorations, stamp paper for wrapping, or assist in baking cookies.

Miniature plastic replicas of fruit or vegetables make perfect adornments for jars of jam or baskets of baking. Match the decoration with an ingredient in your food gift.

Always include the original recipe and preparation directions with your food gift. That way, the recipient can enjoy making it again. It also helps avoid any allergy concerns.

Be sure to label items with any special instructions such as mixing, freezing or chilling information, as well as best-before dates.

Create a gift the whole family can share. Purchase a board game and add a selection of homemade sweet treats or savoury snacks to be enjoyed while playing the game.

Give the gift of time. These days, it seems like everyone could use more of it! Create colourful coupons for babysitting, household chores or yard work. Tuck them into a basket of homemade treats for someone who needs a break.

Keep a few small food gifts wrapped and ready for unexpected company or for a quick hostess gift. Have some frozen treats wrapped and ready to go.

Things to have on hand for homemade gift giving

Simple, inexpensive household, grocery or craft store items make creating Christmas gifts from the kitchen easy and fun. Keep a supply of the following items handy when you start your Christmas gift preparations:

Baskets	Chenille stems	Needles and thread
Bows	Cookie cutters	Pinecones
Boxes	Craft glue	Raffia
Brown lunch bags	Fabric remnants	Ribbon
Buttons	Felt squares	Tape
Candy canes	Florist tape	Tissue paper
Cardboard	Florist wire	Twigs
Cellophane bags	Glue gun	Twine
Cellophane wrap	Hole punch	Wire cutters
Colourful pens	Jingle bells	White or brown paper

Cookies

Cookies are a traditional holiday favourite and make a welcome gift for someone of any age. Here's your chance to help family and friends keep their cookie jar full.

Make and freeze a variety of cookies before the season gets too busy. As soon as the baked cookies have cooled, spread them on a cookie sheet and pop them into the freezer. Once frozen, they can be layered between sheets of waxed paper in an airtight container and stored in the freezer for up to two months. When you're ready to package the cookies, thaw them in the refrigerator (to avoid condensation). If you plan to add

decorations, sanding sugar or sprinkles can be added before baking, but wait until frozen cookies are thawed before adding decorative icing or a light dusting of icing sugar or cocoa.

Before packaging your gift of cookies, put them into a resealable plastic bag or wrap them in plastic wrap to keep them fresh. Then place them in a festive gift bag with tissue paper. Or have your children trace and colour cookie cutter shapes onto brown paper bags. Fill the bags with the cookies, thread the cookie cutters through some ribbons, and tie them onto the bag in a beautiful Christmas bow.

Friendship Cookies

A quick and easy cookie to make. Wrap some in cellophane and put in a North Pole Cookie Tube, below.

Box of chocolate cake mix (2 layer size)	1	1
Cooking oil	1/2 cup	125 mL
Water	1/4 cup	60 mL
Large egg	1	1
White chocolate chips	1 cup	250 mL

Combine first 4 ingredients in large bowl. Add chocolate chips. Mix well. Drop, using 1 tbsp. (15 mL) for each, about 2 inches (5 cm) apart onto greased cookie sheets. Bake in 350°F (175°C) oven for 10 to 12 minutes until set and tops of cookies appear cracked. Do not overbake. Let stand on cookie sheets for 5 minutes before removing to wire racks to cool. Makes 4 dozen (48) cookies.

1 cookie: 85 Calories; 4.6 g Total Fat (2.3 g Mono, 0.9 g Poly, 1.2 g Sat); 5 mg Cholesterol; 11 g Carbohydrate; 0 g Fibre; 1 g Protein; 101 mg Sodium

Pictured on page 12 and on page 174.

✶ North Pole Cookie Tube ✶

Use this gifting idea with any cookie recipe.

MATERIALS
White mailing tube with plastic end-caps
Styrofoam ball (4 inch, 10 cm, diameter)
White craft paint
Wide red ribbon (36 inch, 90 cm, length)
Tissue paper

TOOLS
pencil, ruler, Exacto knife, sponge paintbrush, glue gun

Cut a 7 inch (18 cm) length of the mailing tube. Paint the tube and Styrofoam ball with white paint. Let them dry.

Glue 1 end of the ribbon at an angle to the inside of 1 rim of the tube. Wrap the ribbon at an angle around the tube and glue the end to the inside of the opposite rim. Insert a plastic end-cap into 1 end of the tube. Wrap cookies in cellophane and put inside the tube. Centre the ball on the open end and firmly press onto the tube to seal.

Pictured on page 13.

Eggnog Cookies

Just one of these rich cookies won't be enough. Be sure to include the recipe when you give these away.

Hard margarine (or butter), softened	1/2 cup	125 mL
Granulated sugar	1/2 cup	125 mL
Brown sugar, packed	1/2 cup	125 mL
Large egg	1	1
Eggnog	2/3 cup	150 mL
Brandy (or rum) flavouring	1/2 tsp.	2 mL
All-purpose flour	2 cups	500 mL
Baking soda	1/2 tsp.	2 mL
Ground nutmeg	1/2 tsp.	2 mL
Salt	1/4 tsp.	1 mL
EGGNOG ICING		
Icing (confectioner's) sugar	3/4 cup	175 mL
Eggnog	5 tsp.	25 mL
Hard margarine (or butter), softened	1 tbsp.	15 mL
Ground nutmeg	1/8 tsp.	0.5 mL
Candy sprinkles (or sanding sugar), for decorating		

Cream margarine and both sugars in large bowl. Add egg. Beat well.

Add eggnog and flavouring. Beat until smooth.

Combine next 4 ingredients in medium bowl. Add to eggnog mixture in 2 additions, mixing well after each addition until no dry flour remains. Drop, using 1 tbsp. (15 mL) for each, about 2 inches (5 cm) apart onto ungreased cookie sheets. Bake in 350°F (175°C) oven for 10 to 12 minutes until edges are just golden. Let stand on cookie sheets for 5 minutes before removing to wire racks to cool completely.

Eggnog Icing: Beat first 4 ingredients in small bowl, adding more icing sugar or eggnog if necessary until barely pourable consistency. Makes about 1/3 cup (75 mL) icing. Spoon into paper cone (page 27), or into small resealable freezer bag with tiny piece snipped off corner. Drizzle icing in decorative pattern over each cookie.

Decorate with candy sprinkles. Makes 4 dozen (48) cookies.

1 cookie: 73 Calories; 2.7 g Total Fat (1.6 g Mono, 0.3 g Poly, 0.7 g Sat); 7 mg Cholesterol; 11 g Carbohydrate; trace Fibre; 1 g Protein; 57 mg Sodium

Pictured on page 13.

Photo legend, next page
Left: Friendship Cookies, this page
Top Centre and Bottom Centre: Chocolate Hazelnut Cookies, page 14
Top Right: North Pole Cookie Tube, this page
Right: Eggnog Cookies, above

Chocolate Hazelnut Cookies

This rich, dark cookie is perfect for the chocolate and nut lovers on your list.

Hard margarine (or butter)	1/2 cup	125 mL
Semi-sweet chocolate baking squares (1 oz., 28 g, each), chopped	1 1/2	1 1/2
All-purpose flour	1 1/4 cups	300 mL
Brown sugar, packed	3/4 cup	175 mL
Large eggs, fork-beaten	2	2
Cocoa, sifted if lumpy	2 1/2 tbsp.	37 mL
Coarsely chopped hazelnuts (filberts), toasted (see Tip, page 22) and skins removed (see Tip, page 34)	3/4 cup	175 mL
Milk chocolate chips	1/2 cup	125 mL
White chocolate baking squares (1 oz., 28 g, each), chopped	2	2
Hazelnuts (filberts)	42	42
White chocolate baking squares (1 oz., 28 g, each), chopped	2	2

Heat margarine and semi-sweet chocolate in large heavy saucepan on lowest heat, stirring often until chocolate is almost melted. Do not overheat. Remove from heat. Stir until smooth. Let stand for 5 minutes.

Add next 4 ingredients. Stir until smooth.

Add next 3 ingredients. Mix well. Drop, using 1 tbsp. (15 mL) for each, about 2 inches (5 cm) apart onto greased cookie sheets.

Place 1 hazelnut on top of each mound. Bake in 350°F (175°C) oven for 8 to 10 minutes until just firm. Let stand on cookie sheets for 5 minutes before removing to wire racks to cool.

Heat second amount of white chocolate in small heavy saucepan on lowest heat, stirring often until almost melted. Do not overheat. Remove from heat. Stir until smooth. Spoon into paper cone (page 27), or into small resealable freezer bag with tiny piece snipped off corner. Drizzle chocolate in decorative pattern over each cookie. Let stand until set. May be chilled to speed setting. Makes 3 1/2 dozen (42) cookies.

1 cookie: 105 Calories; 6.4 g Total Fat (3.7 g Mono, 0.5 g Poly, 1.8 g Sat); 11 mg Cholesterol; 11 g Carbohydrate; 1 g Fibre; 2 g Protein; 36 mg Sodium

Pictured on page 12.

Hazelnut Oatmeal Cookies

A creamy hazelnut filling sandwiched between old-fashioned oatmeal cookies. Simply delicious and always welcome as a home-baked gift.

Hard margarine (or butter), softened	1 cup	250 mL
Granulated sugar	1 cup	250 mL
Brown sugar, packed	1 cup	250 mL
Large eggs	2	2
Vanilla	1 1/2 tsp.	7 mL
All-purpose flour	1 1/4 cups	300 mL
Finely chopped hazelnuts (filberts), toasted (see Tip, page 22) and skins removed (see Tip, page 34)	1/3 cup	75 mL
Baking soda	1 tsp.	5 mL
Baking powder	1 tsp.	5 mL
Salt	1/4 tsp.	1 mL
Quick-cooking rolled oats (not instant)	2 3/4 cups	675 mL
Golden raisins (optional)	1 1/2 cups	375 mL
Chocolate hazelnut spread (such as Nutella)	1 1/3 cups	325 mL

Cream margarine and both sugars in large bowl. Add eggs 1 at a time, beating well after each addition. Add vanilla. Beat until smooth.

Combine next 5 ingredients in small bowl. Add to margarine mixture in 2 additions, mixing well after each addition until no dry flour remains.

Add rolled oats and raisins. Mix well. Let stand for 30 minutes. Roll dough into balls, using 1 1/2 tsp. (7 mL) for each. Arrange about 2 inches (5 cm) apart on greased cookie sheets. Bake in 350°F (175°C) oven for about 8 minutes until golden. Let stand on cookie sheets for 5 minutes before removing to wire racks to cool completely.

Spread 1 tsp. (5 mL) hazelnut spread on bottom of 1/2 of cookies. Place remaining 1/2 of cookies on top of filling. Makes 3 1/2 dozen (42) cookies.

1 cookie: 106 Calories; 6.7 g Total Fat (4.3 g Mono, 1.1 g Poly, 1 g Sat); 7 mg Cholesterol; 11 g Carbohydrate; 1 g Fibre; 2 g Protein; 96 mg Sodium

Pictured on page 15.

Top: Jam Jams, page 16
Bottom: Hazelnut Oatmeal Cookies, above

Jam Jams

A pretty addition to a festive tin of cookies!
Sweet raspberry filling peeks through the centres of
these lemon-flavoured treats.

Hard margarine (or butter), softened	1/2 cup	125 mL
Granulated sugar	3/4 cup	175 mL
Egg yolks (large)	3	3
Grated lemon zest	1 1/2 tsp.	7 mL
Lemon juice	1/2 tsp.	2 mL
Vanilla	1/2 tsp.	2 mL
All-purpose flour	1 3/4 cups	425 mL
Baking soda	1/2 tsp.	2 mL
Cream of tartar	1/2 tsp.	2 mL
Raspberry jam	1/2 cup	125 mL
LEMON GLAZE		
Lemon juice	1 tbsp.	15 mL
Icing (confectioner's) sugar	2/3 cup	150 mL

Cream margarine and sugar in large bowl. Add egg yolks 1 at a time, beating well after each addition.

Add next 3 ingredients. Beat until smooth.

Combine flour, baking soda and cream of tartar in medium bowl. Add to margarine mixture in 2 additions, mixing well after each addition until no dry flour remains. Mixture will be crumbly. Shape into ball. Roll out dough between 2 sheets of waxed paper to about 1/8 inch (3 mm) thickness. Discard top sheet of waxed paper. Cut out circles with lightly floured 2 1/2 inch (6.4 cm) round cookie cutter with fluted edge. Roll out scraps to cut more circles. Arrange about 1 inch (2.5 cm) apart on greased cookie sheets. Cut out centre of 1/2 of circles with lightly floured 1 inch (2.5 cm) round or diamond cookie cutter. Bake in 350°F (175°C) oven for about 8 minutes until edges are golden. Let stand on cookie sheets for 5 minutes before removing to wire racks to cool completely.

Spread 1 tsp. (5 mL) jam on bottom of each whole cookie, leaving 1/4 inch (6 mm) edge. Place cookies with cut-out centres on top of jam.

Lemon Glaze: Stir lemon juice into icing sugar in small bowl, adding more lemon juice or icing sugar if necessary until barely pourable consistency. Makes about 1/4 cup (60 mL) glaze. Spoon into paper cone (page 27), or into small resealable freezer bag with tiny piece snipped off corner. Drizzle glaze in decorative pattern over each cookie. Makes 1 1/2 dozen (18) cookies.

1 cookie: 181 Calories; 6.4 g Total Fat (3.8 g Mono, 0.7 g Poly, 1.4 g Sat); 36 mg Cholesterol; 30 g Carbohydrate; 1 g Fibre; 2 g Protein; 104 mg Sodium

Pictured on front cover and on page 15.

JAM JAM WREATHS: Before baking, brush cookies with cut-out centres with fork-beaten egg white. Sprinkle with green sanding (decorating) sugar (see Note). Bake and assemble as directed.

Note: Sanding sugar is a coarse decorating sugar that comes in white and various colours and is available at specialty kitchen stores.

Berry-Full Wafers

An absolutely decadent cookie! So simple to make and give
away in a pretty decorated gift box to someone special.

BERRY FILLING		
Light spreadable strawberry (or raspberry) cream cheese	1/2 cup	125 mL
Icing (confectioner's) sugar	1/2 cup	125 mL
Finely chopped dried cranberries	1/2 cup	125 mL
Raspberry-flavoured liqueur (such as Chambord), optional	1 tsp.	5 mL
Vanilla wafers	72	72
Semi-sweet chocolate baking squares (1 oz., 28 g, each), chopped	12	12
Hard margarine (or butter)	1 tbsp.	15 mL
White chocolate baking square, chopped	1 oz.	28 g

Berry Filling: Combine first 4 ingredients in medium bowl. Makes about 3/4 cup (175 mL) filling.

Spread 1 tsp. (5 mL) filling on bottom of 1/2 of wafers. Place remaining 1/2 of wafers on top of filling. Chill for about 1 hour until filling is firm.

Heat semi-sweet chocolate and margarine in small heavy saucepan on lowest heat, stirring often until chocolate is almost melted. Do not overheat. Remove from heat. Stir until smooth. Place 1 cookie on top of fork. Dip into chocolate mixture until completely coated, allowing excess to drip back into pan. Place on waxed paper-lined cookie sheet. Repeat with remaining cookies and chocolate mixture. Let stand until set. May be chilled to speed setting.

Heat white chocolate in separate small heavy saucepan on lowest heat, stirring often until almost melted. Do not overheat. Remove from heat. Stir until smooth. Spoon into paper cone (page 27), or into small resealable freezer bag with tiny piece snipped off corner. Drizzle chocolate in decorative pattern over each dipped cookie. Let stand until set. Makes 3 dozen (36) cookies.

1 cookie: 101 Calories; 4.6 g Total Fat (1.7 g Mono, 0.4 g Poly, 2.1 g Sat); 5 mg Cholesterol; 15 g Carbohydrate; 1 g Fibre; 1 g Protein; 31 mg Sodium

Pictured on page 10 and on page 19.

Orange Poppy Seed Swirls

Delicate shortbread cookie with a sweet orange filling.
Arrange some in a coloured glass dish
as a gift for your neighbour.

Butter (or hard margarine), softened	1 cup	250 mL
Granulated sugar	1/3 cup	75 mL
Poppy seeds	1 1/2 tbsp.	25 mL
Grated orange zest	1 tbsp.	15 mL
Milk	1 tbsp.	15 mL
All-purpose flour	1 1/2 cups	375 mL
Cornstarch	1/4 cup	60 mL
ORANGE FILLING		
Icing (confectioner's) sugar	1 3/4 cups	425 mL
Hard margarine (or butter), softened	2 tbsp.	30 mL
Orange juice	2 tbsp.	30 mL
Grated orange zest	2 tsp.	10 mL

Cream butter and sugar in medium bowl. Add poppy seeds, orange zest and milk. Beat well.

Combine flour and cornstarch in small bowl. Add to butter mixture in 2 additions, mixing well after each addition until no dry flour remains. Spoon 1/2 of dough into piping bag fitted with medium star tip. Pipe 36 rosettes, 1 1/4 inches (3 cm) in diameter, about 2 inches (5 cm) apart onto greased cookie sheets. Roll remaining dough into thirty-six 3/4 inch (2 cm) balls. Arrange about 2 inches (5 cm) apart on greased cookie sheets. Dip flat-bottomed glass into flour or cornstarch. Flatten balls into 1 1/4 inch (3 cm) diameter discs. Bake rosettes and discs in 350ºF (175ºC) oven for about 10 minutes until golden. Let stand on cookie sheets for 5 minutes before removing to wire racks to cool completely.

Orange Filling: Beat all 4 ingredients in small bowl, adding more icing sugar or orange juice if necessary until spreadable consistency. Makes about 3/4 cup (175 mL) filling. Spread 1 tsp. (5 mL) filling on bottom of each disc. Place rosettes on top of filling. Makes 3 dozen (36) cookies.

1 cookie: 112 Calories; 6.2 g Total Fat (4 g Mono, 0.8 g Poly, 1.3 g Sat);
0 mg Cholesterol; 13 g Carbohydrate; trace Fibre; 1 g Protein; 71 mg Sodium

Pictured on this page.

Roca Cookies

A speckled cookie with creamy caramel filling and almond garnish. Looks pretty and tastes delicious. An ideal gift!

Hard margarine (or butter), softened	1 cup	250 mL
Brown sugar, packed	1/2 cup	125 mL
All-purpose flour	2 cups	500 mL
Salt	1/4 tsp.	1 mL
Finely chopped butter crunch toffee candy (such as Almond Roca)	3/4 cup	175 mL
CARAMEL FILLING		
Granulated sugar	1 cup	250 mL
Water	1/3 cup	75 mL
Hard margarine (or butter)	2 1/2 tbsp.	37 mL
Whipping cream	1/4 cup	60 mL
Whole natural almonds, toasted (see Tip, page 22)	36	36

Cream margarine and brown sugar in large bowl.

Combine flour and salt in small bowl. Add to margarine mixture in 2 additions, mixing well after each addition until no dry flour remains.

Add candy. Mix well. Roll dough into 1 1/4 inch (3 cm) balls. Arrange about 2 inches (5 cm) apart on greased cookie sheets. Dent each with thumb. Bake in 325°F (160°C) oven for about 12 minutes until edges are golden. Remove from oven. Press dents again. Let stand on cookie sheets for 5 minutes before removing to wire racks to cool completely.

Caramel Filling: Heat and stir sugar and water in small saucepan on medium-low for about 10 minutes until sugar is dissolved.

Bring to a boil on medium. Boil gently, uncovered, for 10 to 15 minutes without stirring, brushing side of saucepan with wet pastry brush to dissolve any sugar crystals, until golden brown. Remove from heat.

Carefully add margarine. Mixture may sputter. Stir until margarine is melted.

Carefully add whipping cream. Stir until smooth. Transfer to small heatproof bowl. Let stand for about 15 minutes until cool but still pourable consistency (see Note). Makes about 1/2 cup (125 mL) filling. Spoon 1/2 tsp. (2 mL) filling into dent of each cookie.

Place 1 almond on top of filling on each. Let stand until set. Makes 3 dozen (36) cookies.

1 cookie: 140 Calories; 7.4 g Total Fat (4.6 g Mono, 0.8 g Poly, 1.7 g Sat); 2 mg Cholesterol; 18 g Carbohydrate; trace Fibre; 1 g Protein; 92 mg Sodium

Pictured on page 19.

Note: If caramel begins to harden, microwave, uncovered, on medium-low (30%) for about 10 seconds until pourable consistency.

Top: Roca Cookies, this page
Bottom: Berry-Full Wafers, page 16

Lemon Shortbread Slices

Cookies that look like lemon wedges and melt in your mouth! Perfect in a Tea Break gift basket, page 179, or put a few in a delicate tea cup and saucer to give to your child's teacher.

Butter (or hard margarine), softened	1 cup	250 mL
Granulated sugar	3/4 cup	175 mL
Grated lemon zest	2 tsp.	10 mL
All-purpose flour	2 1/4 cups	550 mL
Egg white (large), fork-beaten	1	1
Yellow sanding (decorating) sugar (see Note)	1/3 cup	75 mL

Cream butter and granulated sugar in large bowl. Add lemon zest. Beat well.

Add flour in 2 additions, mixing well after each addition until no dry flour remains. Roll dough into 3 inch (7.5 cm) diameter log.

Brush log evenly with egg white. Sprinkle sanding sugar evenly on sheet of waxed paper slightly longer than log. Roll log in sanding sugar until coated. Wrap with plastic wrap. Chill for at least 6 hours or overnight. Discard plastic wrap. Cut log into 1/4 inch (6 mm) slices. Cut each slice in half. Arrange halves about 1 inch (2.5 cm) apart on ungreased cookie sheets.

Score each half with knife to make 4 wedges (see line drawing). Bake in 325°F (160°C) oven for 8 to 10 minutes until golden. Let stand on cookie sheets for 5 minutes before removing to wire racks to cool. Makes 6 1/2 dozen (78) cookies.

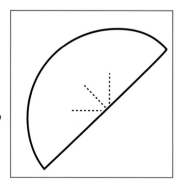

1 cookie: 47 Calories; 2.5 g Total Fat (1.6 g Mono, 0.3 g Poly, 0.5 g Sat);
    0 mg Cholesterol; 6 g Carbohydrate; trace Fibre; 0 g Protein; 30 mg Sodium

Pictured on page 20 and on pages 178/179.

Note: Sanding sugar is a coarse decorating sugar that comes in white and various colours and is available at specialty kitchen stores.

Ditto Chocolate Dips

Chocolate, chocolate, chocolate chip! A rich cookie reminiscent of macaroons. A scrumptious gift for the chocolate lover on your list.

Hard margarine (or butter), softened	1/2 cup	125 mL
Brown sugar, packed	1 cup	250 mL
Large egg	1	1
Vanilla	1 tsp.	5 mL
Quick-cooking rolled oats (not instant)	1 1/2 cups	375 mL
All-purpose flour	1 cup	250 mL
Cocoa, sifted if lumpy	3 tbsp.	50 mL
Baking soda	1/2 tsp.	2 mL
Salt	1/4 tsp.	1 mL
Mini semi-sweet chocolate chips	3/4 cup	175 mL
Semi-sweet (or milk) chocolate melting wafers	1 1/2 cups	375 mL

Cream margarine and brown sugar in large bowl. Add egg. Beat well. Add vanilla. Beat until smooth.

Combine next 5 ingredients in medium bowl. Add to margarine mixture in 2 additions, mixing well after each addition until no dry flour remains.

Add chocolate chips. Mix well. Shape dough into 3 x 7 inch (7.5 x 18 cm) rectangle. Cut in half lengthwise. Wrap each half with plastic wrap. Chill for 3 to 4 hours until firm. Discard plastic wrap from 1 half. Cut crosswise into 1/4 inch (6 mm) slices. Arrange about 1 inch (2.5 cm) apart on greased cookie sheets. Bake in 350°F (175°C) oven for about 10 minutes until firm. Let stand on cookie sheets for 5 minutes before removing to wire racks to cool completely. Repeat with remaining 1/2 of dough.

Heat chocolate wafers in small heavy saucepan on lowest heat, stirring often until almost melted. Do not overheat. Remove from heat. Stir until smooth. Pour into small deep bowl. Dip 1 corner of each cookie straight down into chocolate until about halfway up cookie. Place on waxed paper. Repeat with remaining cookies and chocolate. Let stand until set. May be chilled to speed setting. Makes 4 1/2 dozen (54) cookies.

1 cookie: 90 Calories; 4.4 g Total Fat (2 g Mono, 0.3 g Poly, 1.8 g Sat);
    4 mg Cholesterol; 13 g Carbohydrate; 1 g Fibre; 1 g Protein; 48 mg Sodium

Pictured below.

Nutty Apple Swirls

Attractive, apple pie-flavoured sweets. Mesmerizing cookies that will captivate anyone who receives them!

Basic Sugar Cookie Dough, page 26	1/2 recipe	1/2 recipe
Finely chopped dried apple	1/4 cup	60 mL
Finely chopped pecans	2 tbsp.	30 mL
Brown sugar, packed	2 tbsp.	30 mL
Hard margarine (or butter), melted	2 tbsp.	30 mL
Ground cinnamon	1/4 tsp.	1 mL
Ground ginger	1/4 tsp.	1 mL

Shape Basic Sugar Cookie Dough into 5 inch (12.5 cm) square. Wrap with plastic wrap. Chill for 1 hour. Discard plastic wrap. Roll out dough between 2 sheets of waxed paper to 8 x 10 inch (20 x 25 cm) rectangle. Discard top sheet of waxed paper.

Combine remaining 6 ingredients in small bowl. Spread evenly on dough, leaving 1/2 inch (12 mm) at each long edge. Roll up tightly from long side, jelly roll-style, using waxed paper as guide. Press seam against roll to seal. Wrap with plastic wrap. Chill for about 1 hour until firm. Discard plastic wrap. Place roll, seam-side down, on cutting board. Cut with serrated knife into 1/4 inch (6 mm) slices. Arrange about 1 inch (2.5 cm) apart on greased cookie sheets. Bake in 350°F (175°C) oven for 6 to 8 minutes until just golden. Let stand on cookie sheets for 5 minutes before removing to wire racks to cool. Makes 3 dozen (36) cookies.

1 cookie: 67 Calories; 3.8 g Total Fat (2.4 g Mono, 0.4 g Poly, 0.8 g Sat); 6 mg Cholesterol; 8 g Carbohydrate; trace Fibre; 1 g Protein; 59 mg Sodium

Pictured on page 23.

Tip: To toast nuts, seeds or coconut, spread evenly in shallow pan. Bake in 350°F (175°C) oven for 5 to 10 minutes, stirring or shaking often, until desired doneness.

Lollipop Cookies

Make a cookie bouquet! Wrap these fun-to-eat, minty cookies in clear cellophane and tie the sticks together with ribbon. Or "plant" the cookies in a clay pot filled with colourful jelly beans.

Basic Sugar Cookie Dough, page 26 (see Note)	1/2 recipe	1/2 recipe
Drops of red liquid food colouring	6	6
Lollipop sticks (6 inch, 15 cm, length), cut in half	18	18

Divide Basic Sugar Cookie Dough in half. Roll out 1 half between 2 sheets of waxed paper to 6 x 8 inch (15 x 20 cm) rectangle. Set dough aside.

Add food colouring to second 1/2 of dough in large bowl. Knead in bowl for 1 to 2 minutes until colour is even. Roll out between 2 separate sheets of waxed paper to 6 x 8 inch (15 x 20 cm) rectangle. Discard top sheet of waxed paper from each rolled out dough rectangle. Invert coloured dough onto first rectangle, aligning edges. Press lightly with rolling pin to seal. Discard top sheet of waxed paper. Roll up tightly from long side, jelly roll-style, using waxed paper as guide. Press seam against roll to seal. Wrap with plastic wrap. Chill for at least 6 hours or overnight. Discard plastic wrap. Cut into 1/4 inch (6 mm) slices. Lay 1 slice over 1 lollipop stick on greased cookie sheet, covering about 1 inch (2.5 cm) of stick. Press dough lightly onto stick. Repeat with remaining slices and lollipop sticks, arranging about 1 inch (2.5 cm) apart on greased cookie sheets, alternating direction of sticks. Bake in 350°F (175°C) oven for 6 to 8 minutes until golden. Let stand on cookie sheets for 5 minutes before removing to wire racks to cool. Makes 3 dozen (36) cookies.

1 cookie: 54 Calories; 2.9 g Total Fat (1.8 g Mono, 0.3 g Poly, 0.6 g Sat); 6 mg Cholesterol; 6 g Carbohydrate; trace Fibre; 1 g Protein; 51 mg Sodium

Pictured on page 23.

Note: Omit vanilla from Basic Sugar Cookie Dough. Use the same amount of mint flavouring.

Left and Top Right: Lollipop Cookies, above
Bottom Right: Nutty Apple Swirls, this page

Lemon Almond Snowflakes

Sweet lemon glaze coats these attractive buttery cookies. A sprinkling of white sanding sugar adds sparkle—just like freshly fallen snow!

Butter (not margarine), softened	1 cup	250 mL
Block of almond paste, softened	8 oz.	225 g
Granulated sugar	1/2 cup	125 mL
Grated lemon zest	1 tbsp.	15 mL
Almond flavouring	1/2 tsp.	2 mL
All-purpose flour	2 1/4 cups	550 mL
Sliced blanched almonds, coarsely chopped	1/3 cup	75 mL
SNOWFLAKE GLAZE		
Icing (confectioner's) sugar	2 cups	500 mL
Warm water	3 tbsp.	50 mL
Meringue powder (see Note)	1 tbsp.	15 mL
Lemon juice	2 tsp.	10 mL
White sanding (decorating) sugar (see Note), optional		
Candy sprinkles (optional)		

Beat first 5 ingredients on medium in large bowl for about 10 minutes, scraping down side if necessary, until well combined.

Add flour in 2 additions, mixing well after each addition until no dry flour remains.

Add almonds. Mix well. Divide dough in half. Shape each half into ball. Flatten each ball into disc and wrap with plastic wrap. Chill for 1 hour. Discard plastic wrap from 1 disc. Roll out dough on lightly floured surface to about 1/4 inch (6 mm) thickness. Cut out shapes with lightly floured 2 1/2 to 3 inch (6.4 to 7.5 cm) snowflake cookie cutter. Roll out scraps to cut more snowflakes. Arrange about 2 inches (5 cm) apart on greased cookie sheets. Bake in 350°F (175°C) oven for 6 to 8 minutes until edges are golden. Let stand on cookie sheets for 5 minutes before removing to wire racks to cool completely. Cool cookie sheets between batches. Repeat with remaining disc.

Snowflake Glaze: Beat first 4 ingredients on medium in small bowl for about 5 minutes until thickened. Add more icing sugar or warm water if necessary until barely pourable consistency. Makes about 1 cup (250 mL) glaze. Place sheets of waxed paper under wire racks. Spoon 1/2 tsp. (2 mL) glaze onto each cookie. Spread glaze with back of spoon until cookie is coated, allowing excess to drip onto waxed paper.

Sprinkle each glazed cookie with sanding sugar. Decorate with candy sprinkles. Let stand overnight until set. May be chilled to speed setting. Makes 6 dozen (72) cookies.

1 cookie: 76 Calories; 3.9 g Total Fat (1.5 g Mono, 0.4 g Poly, 1.8 g Sat); 7 mg Cholesterol; 10 g Carbohydrate; 1 g Fibre; 1 g Protein; 29 mg Sodium

Pictured on front cover and on page 25.

Note: Meringue powder can be purchased at specialty kitchen stores or where cake decorating supplies are sold.

Note: Sanding sugar is a coarse decorating sugar that comes in white and various colours and is available at specialty kitchen stores.

Candied Ginger Cookies

Crisp, crackle-topped cookies make a simply delicious gift!

Hard margarine (or butter), softened	1/2 cup	125 mL
Granulated sugar	3/4 cup	175 mL
Egg yolk (large)	1	1
Vanilla	1 tsp.	5 mL
All-purpose flour	1 1/2 cups	375 mL
Minced crystallized ginger	3 tbsp.	50 mL
Baking powder	1 tbsp.	15 mL
Ground ginger	1 tbsp.	15 mL
Ground cinnamon	1 tsp.	5 mL
Ground nutmeg	1/2 tsp.	2 mL
Salt	1/4 tsp.	1 mL
Milk, approximately	3 tbsp.	50 mL

Cream margarine and sugar in large bowl. Add egg yolk. Beat well. Add vanilla. Beat until smooth.

Combine next 7 ingredients in small bowl. Add to margarine mixture in 2 additions, mixing well after each addition until no dry flour remains.

Add enough milk, 1 tbsp. (15 mL) at a time, mixing after each addition until soft dough forms. Roll dough into balls, using 2 tsp. (10 mL) for each. Arrange about 2 inches (5 cm) apart on greased cookie sheets. Bake in 375°F (190°C) oven for 10 to 12 minutes until golden and tops of cookies appear cracked. Let stand on cookie sheets for 5 minutes before removing to wire racks to cool. Makes 2 1/2 dozen (30) cookies.

1 cookie: 79 Calories; 3.5 g Total Fat (2.2 g Mono, 0.4 g Poly, 0.8 g Sat); 7 mg Cholesterol; 11 g Carbohydrate; trace Fibre; 1 g Protein; 96 mg Sodium

Pictured on page 25.

Top: Candied Ginger Cookies, above
Bottom: Lemon Almond Snowflakes, this page

Basic Sugar Cookies

Crisp, with a delightful sugary flavour. A versatile dough to make Nutty Apple Swirls, page 22, Lollipop Cookies, page 22, or Peppermint Patties, page 34. Or simply cut out your favourite shapes and decorate with glaze or sprinkles. Use one of the creative package ideas in our Wrapping It Up section to make a lovely gift.

BASIC SUGAR COOKIE DOUGH

Hard margarine (or butter), softened	1 cup	250 mL
Granulated sugar	1 cup	250 mL
Egg yolks (large)	2	2
Vanilla	1/2 tsp.	2 mL
All-purpose flour	2 1/2 cups	625 mL
Baking powder	1/2 tsp.	2 mL
Salt	1/2 tsp.	2 mL

BASIC COOKIE GLAZE

Icing (confectioner's) sugar	3/4 cup	175 mL
Milk	1 tbsp.	15 mL
Hard margarine (or butter), softened	2 tsp.	10 mL
Vanilla	1/4 tsp.	1 mL
Liquid (or paste) food colouring (see Note)		

Basic Sugar Cookie Dough: Cream margarine and sugar in large bowl. Add egg yolks 1 at a time, beating well after each addition. Add vanilla. Beat until smooth.

Combine flour, baking powder and salt in small bowl. Add to margarine mixture in 2 additions, mixing well after each addition until no dry flour remains. Divide dough in half. Shape each half into ball. Flatten each ball into disc and wrap with plastic wrap. Chill for 1 hour. Discard plastic wrap from 1 disc. Roll out dough between 2 sheets of waxed paper to about 1/8 inch (3 mm) thickness. Discard top sheet of waxed paper. Cut out shapes with lightly floured 2 1/2 inch (6.4 cm) cookie cutters. Roll out scraps to cut more shapes. Arrange about 1 inch (2.5 cm) apart on greased cookie sheets. Bake in 350°F (175°C) oven for 6 to 8 minutes until edges are golden. Let stand on cookie sheets for 5 minutes before removing to wire racks to cool completely. Cool cookie sheets between batches. Repeat with remaining disc.

Basic Cookie Glaze: Beat first 4 ingredients in small bowl, adding more icing sugar or milk if necessary until barely pourable consistency.

Add food colouring 1 drop at a time, stirring well after each addition until desired colour is reached. Makes about 3/4 cup (175 mL) glaze. Spoon into paper cone (page 27), or into small resealable plastic bag with tiny piece snipped off corner. Drizzle glaze over each cookie. Makes 3 dozen (36) cookies.

1 cookie: 120 Calories; 6 g Total Fat (3.8 g Mono, 0.6 g Poly, 1.3 g Sat); 12 mg Cholesterol; 16 g Carbohydrate; trace Fibre; 1 g Protein; 104 mg Sodium

Pictured on pages 28/29.

Note: For best results, use paste food colouring to make bolder colours. Use only a few drops of liquid food colouring to make softer colours.

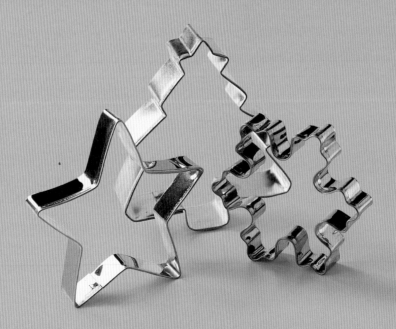

Making A Paper Cone

Paper cones are simple to make and handy in decorating cookies and treats. You can use the cone to pipe fine lines and decorative swirls on cookies, cakes and gingerbread houses.

Cut out a 10 inch (25 cm) square from parchment (or waxed) paper. Fold the square in half diagonally to form a triangle. With your left hand, position the longest side of the triangle vertically, holding it at the centre. Roll up the bottom corner to meet the right corner, turning the point under to form a cone. Hold in position with your right hand.

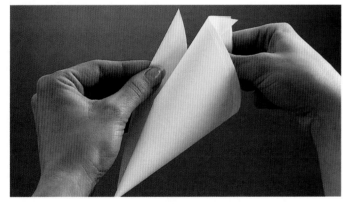

With your left hand, roll the top corner tightly around the cone until it meets the right corner. Tighten the cone to form a sharp tip.

Fold the pointed edges at the top into the cone twice (or secure with a stapler).

Fill the cone 1/3 full with icing or melted chocolate. Pinch the opening together to form a flat edge. Fold the edge down once. Fold the ends to meet in the middle. Fold down again.

Snip a very small piece off the tip of the cone. Start with a small hole—you can always make it bigger.

Photo legend, next page
Top Left: Chocolate Coconut Hearts, page 30
Top Right: Caramel Pecan Cookies, page 30
Bottom Right and Bottom Left: Basic Sugar Cookies, page 26

Chocolate Coconut Hearts

Gift-making made easy! Choose someone on your list whose heart will be warmed by these pretty cookies.

Hard margarine (or butter), softened	1 cup	250 mL
Brown sugar, packed	2/3 cup	150 mL
Large egg	1	1
Vanilla	1 tsp.	5 mL
All-purpose flour	2 cups	500 mL
Fine coconut, toasted (see Tip, page 22)	2/3 cup	150 mL
Cocoa, sifted if lumpy	1/4 cup	60 mL
Milk chocolate melting wafers	1 1/4 cups	300 mL
Fine coconut, toasted (see Tip, page 22)	1/3 cup	75 mL

Cream margarine and brown sugar in large bowl. Add egg and vanilla. Beat until smooth.

Combine flour, first amount of coconut and cocoa in small bowl. Add to margarine mixture in 2 additions, mixing well after each addition until no dry flour remains. Divide dough in half. Shape each half into ball. Flatten each ball into disc and wrap with plastic wrap. Chill for at least 6 hours or overnight. Discard plastic wrap from 1 disc. Roll out dough between 2 sheets of waxed paper to about 1/4 inch (6 mm) thickness. Discard top sheet of waxed paper. Cut out hearts with lightly floured 2 inch (5 cm) heart cookie cutter. Roll out scraps to cut more hearts. Arrange about 1 inch (2.5 cm) apart on greased cookie sheets. Bake in 350°F (175°C) oven for 8 to 10 minutes until firm. Let stand on cookie sheets for 5 minutes before removing to wire racks to cool completely. Cool cookie sheets between batches. Repeat with remaining disc.

Heat chocolate wafers in small heavy saucepan on lowest heat, stirring often until almost melted. Do not overheat. Remove from heat. Stir until smooth. Transfer to small deep bowl.

Measure second amount of coconut into small shallow dish. Dip half of each cookie into chocolate, allowing excess to drip back into bowl. Immediately press dipped cookie half into coconut. Place on wire rack. Repeat with remaining hearts, chocolate and coconut. Let stand until set. May be chilled to speed setting. Makes 5 dozen (60) cookies.

1 cookie: 86 Calories; 5.6 g Total Fat (2.6 g Mono, 0.4 g Poly, 2.3 g Sat); 4 mg Cholesterol; 9 g Carbohydrate; trace Fibre; 1 g Protein; 44 mg Sodium

Pictured on page 28.

Caramel Pecan Cookies

Crunchy pecans, caramel and chocolate make a rich, decadent cookie.

Hard margarine (or butter), softened	1 cup	250 mL
Granulated sugar	1 2/3 cups	400 mL
Brown sugar, packed	1/3 cup	75 mL
Large eggs	3	3
Milk	2 tbsp.	30 mL
Vanilla	2 tsp.	10 mL
All-purpose flour	4 cups	1 L
Baking soda	1 1/2 tsp.	7 mL
Baking powder	1/2 tsp.	2 mL
Salt	1/4 tsp.	1 mL
CARAMEL TOPPING		
Bag of caramels (about 40)	12 oz.	340 g
Milk	2 tbsp.	30 mL
Pecan halves, approximately	2/3 cup	150 mL
Semi-sweet chocolate baking squares (1 oz., 28 g, each), chopped	3	3

Cream margarine and both sugars in large bowl. Add eggs 1 at a time, beating well after each addition.

Add milk and vanilla. Beat until smooth.

Combine next 4 ingredients in separate large bowl. Add to margarine mixture in 4 additions, mixing well after each addition until no dry flour remains. Divide dough in half. Shape each half into ball. Flatten each ball into disc and wrap with plastic wrap. Chill for 1 1/2 hours. Discard plastic wrap from 1 disc. Roll out dough on lightly floured surface to about 1/4 inch (6 mm) thickness. Cut out circles with lightly floured 2 1/2 inch (6.4 cm) round cookie cutter with fluted edge. Roll out scraps to cut more circles. Arrange about 2 inches (5 cm) apart on ungreased cookie sheets. Bake in 350°F (175°C) oven for 8 to 10 minutes until edges are golden. Let stand on cookie sheets for 5 minutes before removing to wire racks to cool completely. Cool cookie sheets between batches. Repeat with remaining disc.

Caramel Topping: Unwrap and place caramels in heavy medium saucepan. Add milk. Heat and stir on medium-low until caramels are melted and mixture is smooth. Reduce heat to low to keep warm. Makes about 1 cup (250 mL) topping. Spread 1 tsp. (5 mL) on each cookie, leaving 1/4 inch (6 mm) edge.

Place 1 pecan half on top of caramel on each. Let stand until set. May be chilled to speed setting.

Heat chocolate in small heavy saucepan on lowest heat, stirring often until almost melted. Do not overheat. Remove from heat. Stir until smooth. Spoon into paper cone (page 27), or into small resealable freezer bag with tiny piece snipped off corner. Drizzle chocolate in decorative pattern over each cookie. Let stand until set. Makes 4 dozen (48) cookies.

1 cookie: 162 Calories; 6.6 g Total Fat (3.7 g Mono, 0.8 g Poly, 1.8 g Sat); 14 mg Cholesterol; 24 g Carbohydrate; 1 g Fibre; 2 g Protein; 127 mg Sodium

Pictured on page 29.

Chipper Crinkle Cookies

A chocolate cookie "snow-kissed" with icing sugar. Ideal to include in a Chocolate Lover's gift basket, page 172.

Hard margarine (or butter), softened	6 tbsp.	100 mL
Granulated sugar	1 cup	250 mL
Large eggs	2	2
Vanilla	1 1/2 tsp.	7 mL
Semi-sweet chocolate chips	1 cup	250 mL
All-purpose flour	1 1/2 cups	375 mL
Baking powder	1 1/2 tsp.	7 mL
Salt	1/4 tsp.	1 mL
Semi-sweet chocolate chips	1 cup	250 mL

Icing (confectioner's) sugar, for dusting

Cream margarine and granulated sugar in large bowl. Add eggs 1 at a time, beating well after each addition. Add vanilla. Beat until smooth.

Heat first amount of chocolate chips in small heavy saucepan on lowest heat, stirring often until almost melted. Do not overheat. Remove from heat. Stir until smooth. Add to margarine mixture. Beat until smooth.

Combine flour, baking powder and salt in small bowl. Add to chocolate mixture in 2 additions, mixing well after each addition until no dry flour remains.

Add second amount of chocolate chips. Mix well. Roll dough into 1 1/2 inch (3.8 cm) balls. Arrange about 1 inch (2.5 cm) apart on greased cookie sheets. Bake in 350°F (175°C) oven for 10 to 12 minutes until edges are firm. Centres may be soft. Let stand on cookie sheets for 5 minutes before removing to wire racks to cool completely.

Using a sieve, dust cookies with icing sugar. Makes 2 1/2 dozen (30) cookies.

1 cookie: 134 Calories; 6.3 g Total Fat (2.8 g Mono, 0.4 g Poly, 2.7 g Sat); 14 mg Cholesterol; 20 g Carbohydrate; 1 g Fibre; 2 g Protein; 71 mg Sodium

Pictured on this page and on page 175.

Brown Sugar And Spice

Two cookie cutter sizes are needed to make these spicy, candy-centred cookies. Make traditional shapes, or try combining different ones. Use a pastry brush to sweep candy crumbs from cookie sheets before baking.

Hard margarine (or butter), softened	1/2 cup	125 mL
Brown sugar, packed	1 cup	250 mL
Large egg	1	1
All-purpose flour	2 cups	500 mL
Baking powder	2 tsp.	10 mL
Ground cinnamon	2 tsp.	10 mL
Ground nutmeg	1 tsp.	5 mL
Salt	1/4 tsp.	1 mL
Crushed hard caramel candies (such as Werther's), or clear hard candies (see Tip, page 34)	1/4 cup	60 mL

Cream margarine and brown sugar in large bowl. Add egg. Beat well.

Combine next 5 ingredients in medium bowl. Add to margarine mixture in 2 additions, mixing well after each addition until no dry flour remains. Divide dough in half. Shape each half into ball. Flatten each ball into disc and wrap with plastic wrap. Let stand for 30 minutes. Discard plastic wrap from 1 disc. Roll out dough on lightly floured surface to about 1/8 inch (3 mm) thickness. Cut out shapes with lightly floured 2 1/2 to 3 inch (6.4 to 7.5 cm) cookie cutter. Roll out scraps to cut more shapes. Arrange about 2 inches (5 cm) apart on parchment paper-lined cookie sheets. Cut out centre of each cookie with lightly floured 1 inch (2.5 cm) cookie cutter.

Spoon 1/2 tsp. (2 mL) candy into cut-out centre of each cookie. Bake in 350ºF (175ºC) oven for 8 to 10 minutes until golden and candy is melted. Let stand on cookie sheets for 10 minutes before removing to wire racks to cool. Cool cookie sheets between batches. Repeat with remaining disc and candy. Makes 2 1/2 dozen (30) cookies.

1 cookie: 100 Calories; 3.5 g Total Fat (2.1 g Mono, 0.4 g Poly, 0.8 g Sat); 7 mg Cholesterol; 16 g Carbohydrate; trace Fibre; 1 g Protein; 88 mg Sodium

Pictured on page 33.

Almond Apricot Yummies

An old-fashioned, crunchy cookie coated in almonds that everyone will love. Put some in a colourful, seasonal tin to give to a friend.

Hard margarine (or butter), softened	1/2 cup	125 mL
Granulated sugar	1/2 cup	125 mL
Egg yolk (large)	1	1
Vanilla	1 tsp.	5 mL
All-purpose flour	1 1/4 cups	300 mL
Salt	1/4 tsp.	1 mL
Ground almonds	1/3 cup	75 mL
Granulated sugar	2 tbsp.	30 mL
Egg white (large)	1	1
Apricot jam, approximately	1/4 cup	60 mL

Cream margarine and first amount of sugar in medium bowl. Add egg yolk. Beat well. Add vanilla. Beat until smooth.

Combine flour and salt in small bowl. Add to margarine mixture in 2 additions, mixing well after each addition until no dry flour remains.

Combine almonds and second amount of sugar in small shallow dish. Set aside.

Beat egg white with fork in small bowl. Set aside. Roll dough into balls, using 1 tbsp. (15 mL) for each. Dip each ball into egg white until coated. Roll each in almond mixture until coated. Arrange about 2 inches (5 cm) apart on greased cookie sheets. Dent each with thumb. Bake in 325ºF (160ºC) oven for about 10 minutes until just golden. Remove from oven. Press dents again. Bake for about 5 minutes until golden. Let stand on cookie sheets for 5 minutes before removing to wire racks to cool.

Spoon 1/2 tsp. (2 mL) jam into each dent. Makes 2 dozen (24) cookies.

1 cookie: 100 Calories; 4.8 g Total Fat (3 g Mono, 0.6 g Poly, 1 g Sat); 9 mg Cholesterol; 13 g Carbohydrate; trace Fibre; 1 g Protein; 76 mg Sodium

Pictured on page 33.

Top: Brown Sugar And Spice, this page
Bottom: Almond Apricot Yummies, above

Almond Smiles

Wish them a Merry Christmas with a smile!
These buttery almond crescents make a fabulous gift.
You might want to double the recipe.

Butter (not margarine), softened	1/2 cup	125 mL
Icing (confectioner's) sugar	1/2 cup	125 mL
Almond flavouring	1/4 tsp.	1 mL
All-purpose flour	1 cup	250 mL
Egg white (large), fork-beaten	1	1
Sliced blanched almonds, chopped	1/2 cup	125 mL
Icing (confectioner's) sugar	1/4 cup	60 mL

Beat butter, first amount of icing sugar and flavouring in medium bowl until well combined.

Add flour. Mix well. Roll dough into 1 inch (2.5 cm) balls. Gently roll each ball into 3 inch (7.5 cm) long log with slightly tapered ends. Brush logs with egg white.

Spread almonds evenly on sheet of waxed paper. Roll each log in almonds until coated. Arrange about 1 inch (2.5 cm) apart on greased cookie sheets, curving ends of each log into crescent shape. Bake in 325°F (160°C) oven for 15 to 18 minutes until just golden.

Immediately sprinkle crescents with second amount of icing sugar until coated. Let stand on cookie sheets for 5 minutes before removing to wire racks to cool. Makes 1 1/2 dozen (18) cookies.

1 cookie: 114 Calories; 7.1 g Total Fat (2.6 g Mono, 0.6 g Poly, 3.5 g Sat); 15 mg Cholesterol; 11 g Carbohydrate; 1 g Fibre; 2 g Protein; 59 mg Sodium

Pictured on page 35.

Tip: To peel hazelnuts, spread toasted nuts on half of tea towel. Fold other half over to cover nuts. Rub vigorously back and forth for 1 to 2 minutes, pressing down until skins are removed. You may not be able to remove all skins of nuts, but outer paper skins should come off.

Peppermint Patties

Sweet peppermint coats thick sugar cookies.
Adds a great minty blast to a gift box of cookies!

Crushed candy canes or hard mint candies (see Tip, below)	3 tbsp.	50 mL
Icing (confectioner's) sugar	3 tbsp.	50 mL
Crushed candy canes or hard mint candies (see Tip, below)	1/4 cup	60 mL
Basic Sugar Cookie Dough, page 26	1/2 recipe	1/2 recipe

Combine first amount of candy and icing sugar in small shallow dish. Set aside.

Add second amount of candy to Basic Sugar Cookie Dough in medium bowl. Mix well. Roll dough into 1 inch (2.5 cm) balls. Arrange about 2 inches (5 cm) apart on greased cookie sheets. Bake in 350°F (175°C) oven for about 10 minutes until just golden. Let stand on cookie sheets for 2 minutes to cool slightly. Press top of each cookie into candy mixture until coated. Place on wire racks to cool. Makes 2 dozen (24) cookies.

1 cookie: 98 Calories; 4.3 g Total Fat (2.7 g Mono, 0.5 g Poly, 0.9 g Sat); 9 mg Cholesterol; 14 g Carbohydrate; trace Fibre; 1 g Protein; 78 mg Sodium

Pictured on front cover and on page 35.

Tip: To crush hard candy, place in large resealable freezer bag. Seal bag. Gently hit with flat side of meat mallet or with rolling pin.

Top: Peppermint Patties, above
Bottom: Almond Smiles, this page

Cookie Sundae Bowls

Wrap these "bowls" in cellophane and include in an Ice Cream Sundae gift basket, page 172. Or fill with your favourite ice cream as a gift to your family. Garnish with cookies cut out of leftover dough.

Hard margarine (not butter), softened	1/4 cup	60 mL
Brown sugar, packed	2/3 cup	150 mL
Large egg	1	1
Vanilla	1 tsp.	5 mL
All-purpose flour	1 1/4 cups	300 mL
Ground almonds	1/4 cup	60 mL
Cocoa, sifted if lumpy	1/4 cup	60 mL
Salt	1/2 tsp.	2 mL
Water		

Cream margarine and brown sugar in large bowl. Add egg. Beat well. Add vanilla. Beat until smooth.

Combine next 4 ingredients in small bowl. Add to margarine mixture in 2 additions, mixing well after each addition until no dry flour remains. Divide dough into 4 equal portions. Shape each portion into ball. Flatten each ball into disc and wrap with plastic wrap. Chill for 1 hour. Invert four 6 oz. (170 mL) ovenproof ramekins onto ungreased cookie sheet. Cover outside of ramekins with foil. Grease foil with cooking spray. Set aside.

Discard plastic wrap from 1 disc. Roll out dough between 2 sheets of waxed paper to about 1/8 inch (3 mm) thickness. Discard top sheet of waxed paper. Cut out 7 flowers with 2 1/2 inch (6.4 cm) flower cookie cutter. Centre 1 flower on foil-covered ramekin to form base.

Dampen edge of second flower with water. Drape over side of ramekin, slightly overlapping base flower. Lightly press edge where flowers meet to seal.

Dampen edge of third flower. Drape over side of ramekin, slightly overlapping base flower and 1 edge of second flower. Lightly press edges to seal. Repeat with remaining 4 flowers, draping each over side of ramekin, around base flower to form tulip-shaped bowl. Repeat with remaining discs and ramekins, for a total of 4 bowls. Bake in 350ºF (175ºC) oven for 12 to 15 minutes until firm. Let stand on cookie sheet on wire rack until cooled. Carefully remove cookie bowl with foil from each ramekin. Gently remove foil. Makes 4 cookie bowls.

1 cookie bowl: 466 Calories; 16.9 g Total Fat (10.2 g Mono, 2 g Poly, 3.6 g Sat); 54 mg Cholesterol; 74 g Carbohydrate; 3 g Fibre; 8 g Protein; 472 mg Sodium

Pictured on page 37 and on page 173.

Florentines

This elegant, lacy cookie with just a hint of citrus will be a pretty gift given in a decorated box.

Brown sugar, packed	1/3 cup	75 mL
Hard margarine (or butter)	1/4 cup	60 mL
Liquid honey	2 tsp.	10 mL
All-purpose flour	1/3 cup	75 mL
Sliced blanched almonds, coarsely chopped	1/3 cup	75 mL
Chopped red glazed cherries	3 tbsp.	50 mL
Diced mixed peel	3 tbsp.	50 mL
Salt	1/4 tsp.	1 mL

Heat and stir brown sugar, margarine and honey in medium saucepan on medium for about 5 minutes until margarine is melted and sugar is dissolved. Remove from heat.

Add remaining 5 ingredients. Mix until no dry flour remains. Drop, using 1 tbsp. (15 mL) for each, about 2 inches (5 cm) apart onto parchment paper-lined cookie sheets. Spread each mound with back of spoon to about 2 inch (5 cm) diameter. Bake in 350ºF (175ºC) oven for about 10 minutes until golden. Let stand on cookie sheets for 10 minutes before removing to wire racks to cool. Makes 12 cookies.

1 cookie: 115 Calories; 5.7 g Total Fat (3.7 g Mono, 0.8 g Poly, 1 g Sat); 0 mg Cholesterol; 16 g Carbohydrate; 1 g Fibre; 1 g Protein; 100 mg Sodium

Pictured on page 37.

Top Left, Bottom Right and Centre Left:
    Cookie Sundae Bowls, this page
Centre: Orange Liqueur Sauce, page 92
Top Right: Florentines, above

Almond Orange Biscotti

So pretty presented in a clear coffee press. Drizzled white chocolate perfectly accents almonds and orange zest in this delightful treat especially made for dunking.

All-purpose flour	3 1/4 cups	800 mL
Granulated sugar	1 cup	250 mL
Slivered almonds, toasted (see Tip, page 22) and coarsely chopped	3/4 cup	175 mL
Grated orange zest	2 tbsp.	30 mL
Baking powder	2 tbsp.	30 mL
Salt	1/4 tsp.	1 mL
Large eggs	4	4
Hard margarine (or butter), melted	2/3 cup	150 mL
White chocolate baking squares (1 oz., 28 g, each), chopped	6	6

Combine first 6 ingredients in large bowl. Make a well in centre.

Beat eggs and margarine with fork in small bowl. Add to well. Mix until soft dough forms. Turn out onto lightly floured surface. Knead 6 times. Divide dough in half. Roll each half into 10 inch (25 cm) long log. Place about 2 inches (5 cm) apart on greased cookie sheet. Flatten each log slightly. Bake in 375°F (190°C) oven for about 25 minutes until golden. Let stand on cookie sheet for about 20 minutes until cool enough to handle. Cut each log diagonally with serrated knife into 1/2 inch (12 mm) slices. Arrange evenly spaced apart on greased cookie sheets. Bake in 350°F (175°C) oven for about 15 minutes, turning once at halftime, until dry and crisp. Let stand on cookie sheets for 5 minutes before removing to wire racks to cool completely.

Heat chocolate in small heavy saucepan on lowest heat, stirring often until almost melted. Do not overheat. Remove from heat. Stir until smooth. Spoon into paper cone (page 27), or into small resealable freezer bag with tiny piece snipped off corner. Drizzle chocolate in decorative pattern over 1 side of each slice. Let stand until set. May be chilled to speed setting. Makes 2 1/2 dozen (30) biscotti.

1 biscotti: 179 Calories; 8.6 g Total Fat (4.8 g Mono, 1 g Poly, 2.3 g Sat); 30 mg Cholesterol; 23 g Carbohydrate; 1 g Fibre; 3 g Protein; 158 mg Sodium

Pictured on page 39.

Cranberry Almond Biscotti

Traditional biscotti in miniature! Place in a clear jar decorated with a festive ribbon and give to the coffee lover on your list.

All-purpose flour	1 3/4 cups	425 mL
Granulated sugar	2/3 cup	150 mL
Baking powder	1/2 tsp.	2 mL
Salt	1/4 tsp.	1 mL
Hard margarine (or butter), softened	1/3 cup	75 mL
Large eggs	2	2
Almond flavouring	1/2 tsp.	2 mL
Dried cranberries	2/3 cup	150 mL
Whole natural almonds	2/3 cup	150 mL

Combine first 4 ingredients in large bowl. Cut in margarine until mixture resembles coarse crumbs. Make a well in centre.

Beat eggs and flavouring with fork in small bowl. Add to well. Mix until stiff dough forms. Turn out onto lightly floured surface. Shape dough into ball. Flatten slightly.

Sprinkle cranberries and almonds over top. Press down lightly. Fold dough in half to enclose cranberries and almonds. Knead for 1 to 2 minutes until evenly distributed. Divide dough into 4 equal portions. Roll each portion into 6 inch (15 cm) long log. Place about 2 inches (5 cm) apart on same greased cookie sheet. Flatten each log slightly. Bake in 350°F (175°C) oven for about 20 minutes until golden. Let stand on cookie sheet for about 20 minutes until cool enough to handle. Cut each log diagonally with serrated knife into 1/2 inch (12 mm) slices. Arrange evenly spaced apart on greased cookie sheets. Bake in 300°F (150°C) oven for about 20 minutes, turning once at halftime, until dry and crisp. Let stand on cookie sheets for 5 minutes before removing to wire racks to cool. Makes 3 1/2 dozen (42) biscotti.

1 biscotti: 66 Calories; 3 g Total Fat (1.8 g Mono, 0.5 g Poly, 0.5 g Sat); 10 mg Cholesterol; 9 g Carbohydrate; 1 g Fibre; 1 g Protein; 40 mg Sodium

Pictured on page 39.

Left: Almond Orange Biscotti, this page
Right: Cranberry Almond Biscotti, above

Dry Mixes

These clever, unique mixes bring a real touch of home to the holiday season. With so many practical recipes to choose from, it will be easy to find the perfect gift for that special person on your list: handy muffin mixes for the busy mom, exceptional tea and hot chocolate mixes for the outdoor enthusiast, and even zesty spice rubs for the grilling expert!

Except for the "all-inclusive" kits, which should be used within ten days of giving, these wonderful mixes can be made ahead of time. Start early—plan to assemble these recipes up to six weeks in advance and include a "best-before" date on the gift,

allowing about one month of shelf life. Pack the mixes into a variety of decorative jars and containers. You can maintain the visual effect of layered mixes by tightly packing tissue or cellophane in the jar's headspace so that the contents remain undisturbed.

Let your imagination guide you as you wrap up these gifts. Don't forget to photocopy or write out the directions for use and attach them to your gift. Think about including the original recipe too. You just might be passing on a tradition for someone else to start.

G-Rated Punch Mix

*So many ways to layer this attractive mix.
A smart gift for a grandmother or an aunt. And don't
forget to add a jar to a Snack Attack gift basket, page 177.*

Envelope of unsweetened purple powdered drink crystals	1/4 oz.	6 g
Granulated sugar	1 cup	250 mL
Drops of red liquid food colouring	4	4
Drops of blue liquid food colouring	4	4
Envelope of unsweetened orange powdered drink crystals	1/4 oz.	6 g
Granulated sugar	1 cup	250 mL
Drops of yellow liquid food colouring	8	8
Envelope of unsweetened green powdered drink crystals	1/4 oz.	6 g
Granulated sugar	1 cup	250 mL
Drops of green liquid food colouring	8	8
Envelope of unsweetened red powdered drink crystals	1/4 oz.	6 g
Granulated sugar	1 cup	250 mL
Drops of red liquid food colouring	8	8

Combine first 4 ingredients in jar with tight-fitting lid. Shake until colour is even. Spread evenly on sheet of waxed paper. Let stand for about 1 hour until dry. Pour sugar mixture through sieve into small bowl. Discard lumps from sieve.

Repeat with next 3 ingredients to make orange sugar. Dry on separate sheet of waxed paper. Pour through sieve into separate small bowl.

Repeat with next 3 ingredients to make green sugar. Dry on separate sheet of waxed paper. Pour through sieve into separate small bowl.

Repeat with remaining 3 ingredients to make red sugar. Dry on separate sheet of waxed paper. Pour through sieve into separate small bowl. Spoon equal amounts of each coloured sugar, alternating in several layers, into small jars with tight-fitting lids. If desired, tilt jar or use wooden spoon handle to create uneven, decorative layering effect. Makes about 4 cups (1 L).

Pictured on this page and on page 177.

Directions for G-Rated Punch:

Measure 1/4 cup (60 mL) G-Rated Punch Mix into small pitcher. Add 2 cups (500 mL) lemon lime soft drink and 2 cups (500 mL) club soda. Stir gently until mix is dissolved. Makes about 4 cups (1 L).

1 cup (250 mL): 51 Calories; 0 g Total Fat (0 g Mono, 0 g Poly, 0 g Sat); 0 mg Cholesterol; 13 g Carbohydrate; 0 g Fibre; 0 g Protein; 0 mg Sodium

Mulled Cider Spice Pouch

A sweet and spicy gift! Include in a gift basket with a bottle of apple cider or juice, a couple of mugs and extra cinnamon sticks for stirring.

Cinnamon sticks (4 inches, 10 cm, each), broken up	3	3
Chopped dried apple	2 tbsp.	30 mL
Whole allspice	1 tbsp.	15 mL
Dried orange peel (see Note)	2 tsp.	10 mL
Aniseed	1 tsp.	5 mL
Whole cloves	1 tsp.	5 mL
Cheesecloth		

Combine first 6 ingredients in small bowl. Put spice mixture in centre of 8 inch (20 cm) square of double-layered cheesecloth. Draw up corners and tie with butcher's string. Makes 1 spice pouch.

Pictured on page 43.

Note: Omit dried orange peel. Use same amount of dried zest. To make dried zest, spread zest from 1 medium orange in greased shallow pan. Bake in 200°F (95°C) oven for about 15 minutes until dry. Store any remaining dried zest in jar with tight-fitting lid.

Directions for Mulled Cider:

Pour 6 cups (1.5 L) apple cider (or juice) into medium saucepan. Place Mulled Cider Spice Pouch in apple cider. Bring to a boil on medium. Reduce heat to medium-low. Cover. Simmer for 15 minutes to blend flavours. Discard spice pouch. Makes about 6 cups (1.5 L).

1 cup (250 mL): 123 Calories; 0.3 g Total Fat (0 g Mono, 0.1 g Poly, 0.1 g Sat); 0 mg Cholesterol; 31 g Carbohydrate; trace Fibre; 0 g Protein; 8 mg Sodium

---

Mulled Wine Kit

Something special to bring to a seasonal dinner and share with friends. Or give this in a Stress Buster gift basket, page 179.

Medium orange	1	1
Cinnamon sticks (4 inches, 10 cm, each), broken up	2	2
Whole green cardamom, bruised (see Tip, page 46)	8	8
Whole cloves	12	12
Brown sugar, packed	1/3 cup	75 mL
Coarsely chopped crystallized ginger	1/4 cup	60 mL
Bottle of burgundy (or alcohol-free red) wine	26 oz.	750 mL

Place orange in large decorative container or jar with lid.

Put cinnamon sticks, cardamom and cloves into small decorative container with lid. Place inside large container with orange. Cover with lid.

Combine brown sugar and ginger in small bowl. Spoon into medium decorative container or jar with tight-fitting lid. Place on top of large container. Tie with ribbon. Add bottle of wine. Makes 1 kit.

Pictured on page 43 and on page 178.

Directions for Mulled Wine:

Pour wine into large saucepan. Cut orange in half. Squeeze juice from 1 orange half into wine. Add squeezed orange half and brown sugar mixture to wine mixture. Heat and stir on medium until brown sugar is dissolved. Reduce heat to medium-low. Add spices. Cover. Simmer for 20 minutes. Do not overheat. Strain wine mixture through sieve into heatproof pitcher. Discard spices and orange half. Pour into 4 small warmed mugs. Cut remaining orange half into thin slices. Garnish each mug with orange slices. Makes about 2 2/3 cups (650 mL). Serves 4.

1 serving: 234 Calories; 0.1 g Total Fat (0 g Mono, 0 g Poly, 0 g Sat); 0 mg Cholesterol; 29 g Carbohydrate; trace Fibre; 1 g Protein; 20 mg Sodium

---

Left: Mulled Wine Kit, this page
Centre Right: Caramel Cinnamon Stir Sticks, page 72
Bottom Right: Mulled Cider Spice Pouch, this page

Snowman-In-A-Mug Mix

Mint candy adds fresh, frosty flavour to this creamy white chocolate drink. Delightfully different! Give it in a Snowman Jar, page 45, or include it in a Kid's Best Friend gift basket, page 172.

Skim milk powder	2 cups	500 mL
White hot chocolate mix	1 cup	250 mL
Powdered coffee whitener	1/2 cup	125 mL
Candy cane pieces (or hard mint candies)	1/4 cup	60 mL
Miniature marshmallows	1 cup	250 mL
Candy canes (or candy sticks), 4 inches (10 cm) each, for garnish	4	4

Process first 4 ingredients in blender or food processor until fine powder. Transfer to large bowl.

Add marshmallows. Stir well. Spoon into jar with tight-fitting lid. Tie candy canes with raffia or ribbon to jar. Makes about 4 cups (1 L).

Pictured on page 45.

Directions for Snowman-In-A-Mug:

Spoon 3 to 4 tbsp. (50 to 60 mL) Snowman-In-A-Mug Mix into each of 4 large mugs. Add 3/4 cup (175 mL) boiling water. Stir. Garnish each with 1 candy cane for stirring. Serves 4.

1 serving: 148 Calories; 1.4 g Total Fat (0.2 g Mono, 0 g Poly, 1.1 g Sat); 2 mg Cholesterol; 32 g Carbohydrate; 0 g Fibre; 5 g Protein; 103 mg Sodium

---

Soothing Tummy Tea Mix

This fragrant, soothing blend is perfect after a big Christmas dinner or when the holidays get hectic! Package with a delicate teacup and infuser ball, or add it to a Tea Break gift basket, page 179.

Dried mint leaves	1/4 cup	60 mL
Dried rosemary, crushed	1 tsp.	5 mL
Dried sage	1 tsp.	5 mL
Dried orange peel (see Note)	1/2 tsp.	2 mL

Combine all 4 ingredients in small bowl. Spoon into decorative jar with tight-fitting lid. Makes about 1/3 cup (75 mL).

Pictured below and on pages 178/179.

Note: Omit dried orange peel. Use same amount of dried zest. To make dried zest, spread zest from 1 medium orange in greased shallow pan. Bake in 200ºF (95ºC) oven for about 15 minutes until dry. Store remaining dried zest in jar with tight-fitting lid.

Directions for Soothing Tummy Tea:

Measure 2 tsp. (10 mL) Soothing Tummy Tea Mix into infuser ball. Place in 2 cup (500 mL) teapot. Pour 1 cup (250 mL) boiling water into teapot. Cover. Let steep for 2 minutes. Makes about 1 cup (250 mL).

1 cup (250 mL): 0 Calories; 0 g Total Fat (0 g Mono, 0 g Poly, 0 g Sat); 0 mg Cholesterol; 0 g Carbohydrate; 0 g Fibre; 0 g Protein; 0 mg Sodium

---

❋ Snowman Jar ❋

Although any warm drink mix can be given in this festive jar, the Snowman-In-A-Mug Mix is ideal.

MATERIALS

Red felt piece (9 × 12 inches, 22 × 30 cm)
Florist wire (24 gauge), 5 1/2 inch (14 cm) length
White felt piece (9 × 12 inches, 22 × 30 cm)
White pompom (3/4 inch, 2 cm, diameter)
Small jar with lid (1/2 pint, 250 mL, size)
Styrofoam ball (3 inch, 7.5 cm, diameter)
Small white sock (size 7-9)
2 craft eyes (1/2 inch, 1.2 cm, diameter)
Craft carrot (1 1/2 inch, 3.8 cm, length)
5 black pompoms (1/4 inch, 0.6 cm, diameter)
3 coloured buttons (1/2 inch, 1.2 cm, diameter)
Small wrapped candy cane (2 1/2 inches, 6.4 cm)

TOOLS

scissors, white craft glue, sewing needle, red thread, pinking shears, white thread

Cut one 1 × 9 inch (2.5 × 22 cm) strip of red felt to make a scarf. Cut small slits along both ends to make a fringe.

Enlarge the hat pattern 400%. Fold the remaining red felt in half. Lay the long side of the pattern on the fold, and pin in place. Cut out the pattern, being careful not to cut the fold. Unfold the felt.

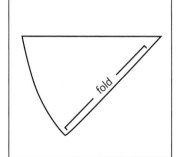

Glue the florist wire along 1 straight edge of the hat, about 1/4 inch (0.6 cm) from the edge. Align the straight edges evenly with the wire inside. Sew the edges together with red thread.

With pinking shears, cut one 1/2 × 9 inch (1.2 × 22 cm) strip of white felt for the hat trim. Glue, scalloped-edge up, along the bottom edge of the hat. Glue a white pompom to the top of the hat at its peak.

Fill the jar with 1 cup (250 mL) Snowman-In-A-Mug Mix, page 44, and seal with the lid.

Cut a small piece from the Styrofoam ball so it will sit flat on the lid. Put the jar, bottom-end down, inside the sock. Place the ball, flat-side down, on top of the lid.

Pull the sock up and over the ball. Position the heel of the sock where the ball meets the lid. Sew the sock closed at the top of the ball using white thread. Trim the sock near the stitching, leaving about a 1/2 inch (1.2 cm) seam allowance.

Glue the eyes, carrot and a smile of black pompoms to the head of the snowman. Glue the buttons to the body. Tie the scarf around the snowman's neck. Glue the candy cane onto 1 side of the body. Top with the hat.

Pictured below.

*Centre Left: Snowman Jar, this page
Bottom Right: Snowman-In-A-Mug, page 44*

Hot Chocolate Mix

Rich chocolate accented with sweet marshmallows and a dash of cinnamon. A simply sensational gift on its own, or given in a decorative jar along with a mug or in a Chocolate Lover's gift basket, page 172.

Miniature marshmallows	1/4 cup	60 mL
Dark chocolate bars (3 1/2 oz., 100 g, each), coarsely chopped	2	2
Ground cinnamon	1/2 tsp.	2 mL

Layer all 3 ingredients, in order given, in jar with tight-fitting lid. Makes about 1 1/4 cups (300 mL).

Pictured on page 47 and on page 175.

Directions for Hot Chocolate:

Heat 4 cups (1 L) milk in heavy medium saucepan on medium until hot and bubbles form around edge of saucepan. Remove from heat. Add contents of jar. Heat and stir on low for about 5 minutes until smooth. Serves 4.

1 serving: 239 Calories; 10.3 g Total Fat (3.3 g Mono, 0.4 g Poly, 6.1 g Sat); 10 mg Cholesterol; 31 g Carbohydrate; 2 g Fibre; 10 g Protein; 133 mg Sodium

---

Pictured on page 47.

Tip: Cardamom is a spicy, sweet spice that comes both ground or whole in the pod. To bruise cardamom, hit pods with mallet or press with flat side of wide knife until they crack open slightly.

Amaretto Mochaccino Mix

Simply stirred in a mug or processed until frothy, this fragrant hot beverage is sure to please. Include this mix in the Good Neighbour gift basket, page 184.

Brown sugar, packed	1/2 cup	125 mL
Almond flavouring	2 tsp.	10 mL
Salt	1/4 tsp.	1 mL
Skim milk powder	1 cup	250 mL
Cocoa, sifted if lumpy	1/2 cup	125 mL
Powdered coffee whitener	2/3 cup	150 mL
Instant coffee granules	1/3 cup	75 mL

Combine first 3 ingredients in small bowl. Spoon into jar with tight-fitting lid.

Layer remaining 4 ingredients, in order given, on top of brown sugar mixture in jar. Makes about 2 2/3 cups (650 mL).

Pictured on page 47 and on page 184.

Directions for Amaretto Mochaccino:

Stir contents of jar before measuring. Measure 1/4 to 1/3 cup (60 to 75 mL) Amaretto Mochaccino Mix into small mug. Add 1 cup (250 mL) boiling water or hot milk. Stir until mix is dissolved. For a fancier hot beverage, carefully process Mix and hot liquid in blender until frothy. Pour into mug. Top with whipped cream and chocolate sprinkles, if desired. Makes about 1 cup (250 mL).

1 cup (250 mL): 134 Calories; 2.9 g Total Fat (0.3 g Mono, 0 g Poly, 2.5 g Sat); 2 mg Cholesterol; 24 g Carbohydrate; 1 g Fibre; 6 g Protein; 137 mg Sodium

Pictured on page 47.

Directions for Double Amaretto Mochaccino:

Add 1 to 2 tbsp. (15 to 30 mL) almond-flavoured liqueur (such as Amaretto). Stir and enjoy!

Top Left: Amaretto Mochaccino, above
Top Right: Amaretto Mochaccino Mix, this page
Bottom Right: Hot Chocolate, this page
Bottom Left: Hot Chocolate Mix, this page

Mushroom Risotto Mix

Earthy mushrooms and savoury seasonings make this cheesy risotto especially good. Present it to someone in a decorated jar or in an Italian gift basket, page 182.

Arborio rice	3/4 cup	175 mL
Parsley flakes	1 tbsp.	15 mL
Dried mint leaves	2 tsp.	10 mL
Chicken bouillon powder	2 tbsp.	30 mL
Lemon pepper	1/2 tsp.	2 mL
Dried chives	2 tbsp.	30 mL
Arborio rice	3/4 cup	175 mL
Package of dried porcini mushrooms	3/4 oz.	22 g

Layer first 7 ingredients, in order given, in 4 cup (1 L) jar with tight-fitting lid.

Put mushrooms in decorative cellophane bag. Place on top of rice in jar. Makes about 4 cups (1 L).

Pictured on page 49 and on page 182.

Directions for Mushroom Risotto:

Put mushrooms into small bowl. Cover with warm water. Let stand for 10 minutes. Drain. Bring 4 1/2 cups (1.1 L) water to a boil in small saucepan. Reduce heat to low. Cover. Measure 1 cup (250 mL) cold water and 1 tbsp. (15 mL) hard margarine or butter into medium saucepan. Bring to a boil. Reduce heat to medium. Add softened mushrooms and remaining contents of jar, stirring constantly until liquid is almost absorbed. Add hot water 1/2 cup (125 mL) at a time, stirring after each addition until water is absorbed. Mixture should be moist and creamy and rice should be tender. Add 1/2 cup (125 mL) grated Parmesan cheese. Stir well. Serves 6.

1 serving: 290 Calories; 5.6 g Total Fat (2.4 g Mono, 0.6 g Poly, 2.3 g Sat); 7 mg Cholesterol; 50 g Carbohydrate; 1 g Fibre; 10 g Protein; 943 mg Sodium

---

Parmesan Herb Focaccia Mix

This flatbread mix bakes up golden, dimpled and delicious. It is a welcome hostess gift when invited to dinner. Complete your gift with jars of olive oil and balsamic vinegar, and some small plates for dipping.

All-purpose flour	2 1/2 cups	625 mL
Envelope of instant yeast (or 2 1/4 tsp., 11 mL)	1	1
Dried chives	2 tsp.	10 mL
Italian seasoning	1 1/2 tsp.	7 mL
Granulated sugar	1/2 tsp.	2 mL
Salt	1/2 tsp.	2 mL

Combine all 6 ingredients in medium bowl. Spoon into decorative airtight container. Makes about 2 1/2 cups (625 mL).

Directions for Parmesan Herb Focaccia:

Combine Parmesan Herb Focaccia Mix and 1/3 cup (75 mL) grated Parmesan cheese in large bowl. Make a well in centre. Add 1 cup (250 mL) plus 2 tbsp. (30 mL) very warm water and 1 tbsp. (15 mL) olive oil to well. Mix until soft dough forms. Turn out onto lightly floured surface. Knead for 5 to 10 minutes until smooth and elastic. Cover dough with inverted bowl. Let stand for 10 minutes. Roll out dough and press in greased 12 inch (30 cm) pizza pan. Brush top of dough with olive oil. Cover with greased waxed paper and tea towel. Let stand in oven with light on and door closed for about 1 hour until doubled in size. Poke indentations into dough with fingertips. Drizzle 1 tbsp. (15 mL) olive oil evenly over dough. Oil will pool in indentations. Sprinkle with 1/3 cup (75 mL) grated Parmesan cheese. Bake in 425°F (220°C) oven for 15 to 20 minutes until golden. Cuts into 12 wedges.

1 wedge: 155 Calories; 4.4 g Total Fat (2.2 g Mono, 0.4 g Poly, 1.5 g Sat); 5 mg Cholesterol; 23 g Carbohydrate; 1 g Fibre; 6 g Protein; 258 mg Sodium

---

Pictured on page 49.

Top Left and Bottom Left: Parmesan Herb Focaccia, above
Centre: Mushroom Risotto Mix, this page
Right: Raspberry Thyme Vinegar, page 91

Biscuit Mix

A simple mix for tender biscuits to send to a student in a College Care Package, page 176. Use the mix to make Cheese Biscuits or Quick Crustless Quiche, too.

All-purpose flour	6 cups	1.5 L
Baking powder	4 1/2 tbsp.	67 mL
Granulated sugar	1 tbsp.	15 mL
Salt	1 1/2 tsp.	7 mL
Cooking oil	1 cup	250 mL

Combine first 4 ingredients in large bowl.

Add cooking oil in thin stream while beating on low until mixture resembles coarse crumbs. Spoon into decorative cellophane bag or airtight container. Makes about 8 cups (2 L).

Pictured below and on page 176 .

Top: Biscuit Mix, above
Bottom: Cheese Biscuits, this page

Directions for Biscuits:

Measure 2 cups (500 mL) Biscuit Mix into medium bowl. Make a well in centre. Add 2/3 cup (150 mL) milk to well. Stir until just moistened. Drop, using 2 tbsp. (30 mL) for each, about 2 inches (5 cm) apart onto greased baking sheet. Bake in 400ºF (205ºC) oven for 12 to 14 minutes until just golden. Serve warm. Makes about 12 biscuits.

1 biscuit: 110 Calories; 5.2 g Total Fat (2.9 g Mono, 1.5 g Poly, 0.5 g Sat); 1 mg Cholesterol; 14 g Carbohydrate; 1 g Fibre; 2 g Protein; 155 mg Sodium

Directions for Cheese Biscuits:

Combine 2 cups (500 mL) Biscuit Mix and 3/4 cup (175 mL) grated sharp Cheddar cheese in medium bowl. Make a well in centre. Add 2/3 cup (150 mL) milk to well. Stir until just moistened. Drop, using 2 tbsp. (30 mL) for each, about 2 inches (5 cm) apart onto greased baking sheet. Bake in 400ºF (205ºC) oven for 12 to 14 minutes until just golden. Serve warm. Makes about 12 cheese biscuits.

1 cheese biscuit: 141 Calories; 7.6 g Total Fat (3.6 g Mono, 1.6 g Poly, 2 g Sat); 8 mg Cholesterol; 14 g Carbohydrate; 1 g Fibre; 4 g Protein; 232 mg Sodium

Pictured on this page.

Directions for Quick Crustless Quiche:

Combine 1 cup (250 mL) diced cooked ham and 1 cup (250 mL) grated Monterey Jack cheese in medium bowl. Spread evenly in greased 9 inch (22 cm) pie plate. Process 1 cup (250 mL) milk, 1/2 cup (125 mL) Biscuit Mix, 1/2 cup (125 mL) chopped onion and 3 large eggs in blender until smooth. Pour over ham mixture. Bake in 350ºF (175ºC) oven for 40 to 45 minutes until knife inserted in centre comes out clean. Let stand for 10 minutes. Cuts into 6 wedges.

1 wedge: 243 Calories; 14 g Total Fat (5.4 g Mono, 1.7 g Poly, 6 g Sat); 143 mg Cholesterol; 12 g Carbohydrate; trace Fibre; 17 g Protein; 634 mg Sodium

Top Left: "Rhuby" Ginger Marmalade, page 84

Top Right and Bottom: Sesame Health Loaf, below

Sesame Health Loaf Mix

This bran and sesame quick bread mix becomes a satisfying, nutritious loaf with a slightly sweet flavour. Give with a jar of "Rhuby" Ginger Marmalade, page 84.

Whole wheat flour	1 1/4 cups	300 mL
Wheat germ	1 tbsp.	15 mL
All-purpose flour	1/2 cup	125 mL
Sesame seeds	2 tbsp.	30 mL
Baking powder	1 tsp.	5 mL
Salt	1/2 tsp.	2 mL
All-bran cereal	2 cups	500 mL

Combine whole wheat flour and wheat germ in small bowl. Spoon into large jar with tight-fitting lid.

Combine next 4 ingredients in same small bowl. Spoon on top of flour mixture.

Measure cereal into decorative cellophane bag. Place on top of sesame seed mixture in jar. Makes about 5 cups (1.25 L).

Directions for Sesame Health Loaf:

Combine all-bran cereal and 1 1/2 cups (375 mL) milk in medium bowl. Let stand for about 10 minutes until milk is absorbed. Add 3 large, fork-beaten eggs and 1/3 cup (75 mL) liquid honey. Mix well. Set aside. Empty remaining contents of jar into large bowl. Stir. Make a well in centre. Add cereal mixture to well. Stir until just moistened. Spread evenly in greased 9 x 5 x 3 inch (22 x 12.5 x 7.5 cm) loaf pan. Bake in 350°F (175°C) oven for 50 to 55 minutes until wooden pick inserted in centre comes out clean. Cuts into 16 slices.

1 slice: 129 Calories; 2.2 g Total Fat (0.7 g Mono, 0.5 g Poly, 0.6 g Sat); 41 mg Cholesterol; 26 g Carbohydrate; 4 g Fibre; 5 g Protein; 202 mg Sodium

Pictured above.

Calico Bean Soup Mix

This wholesome soup mix can be given with a container of chicken bouillon powder and can of diced tomatoes, or with the Boston Brown Loaves Mix, this page. A hungry student will also welcome it in a College Care Package, page 176.

Dried black beans	1/2 cup	125 mL
Dried baby lima beans	1/2 cup	125 mL
Dried red kidney beans	1/2 cup	125 mL
Dried navy beans	1/2 cup	125 mL
Bay leaf	1	1
Chili powder	1 tsp.	5 mL
Garlic powder	1/2 tsp.	2 mL
Dried whole oregano	1/2 tsp.	2 mL
Dried thyme	1/2 tsp.	2 mL
Dried basil	1/2 tsp.	2 mL
Pepper	1/2 tsp.	2 mL

Layer first 4 ingredients, in order given, in jar with tight-fitting lid.

Combine remaining 7 ingredients in small cup. Spoon into decorative cellophane bag. Place on top of beans in jar. Makes about 2 cups (500 mL).

Pictured on page 53.

Directions for Calico Bean Soup:

Remove bag from jar. Set aside. Empty remaining contents of jar into sieve. Rinse and drain beans. Transfer to large pot or Dutch oven. Add 6 cups (1.5 L) water. Bring to a boil on high. Remove from heat. Cover. Let stand for 1 hour. Drain. Add contents of spice bag and 9 cups (2.25 L) water. Stir. Bring to a boil on high. Reduce heat to medium-low. Cover. Simmer for about 1 1/4 hours, stirring occasionally, until beans are tender. Add 14 oz. (398 mL) can of diced tomatoes (with juice) and 3 tbsp. (50 mL) chicken bouillon powder. Stir. Cover. Simmer for 20 minutes to blend flavours. Discard bay leaf. Makes about 11 cups (2.75 L).

1 cup (250 mL): 120 Calories; 1 g Total Fat (0.2 g Mono, 0.4 g Poly, 0.2 g Sat); 0 mg Cholesterol; 21 g Carbohydrate; 5 g Fibre; 8 g Protein; 598 mg Sodium

---

Boston Brown Loaves Mix

A great gift for someone who loves to bake. Place in a basket with seven 3 inch (7.5 cm) diameter clay pots. Be sure to add a copy of the ingredients so they can make these tasty loaves again!

Yellow cornmeal	1 1/4 cups	300 mL
Whole wheat flour	1 cup	250 mL
Rye flour	1 cup	250 mL
Baking soda	1 tsp.	5 mL
Salt	1 tsp.	5 mL
Dark raisins	1/2 cup	125 mL
Golden raisins	1/2 cup	125 mL
Fancy (mild) molasses	2/3 cup	150 mL

Combine first 5 ingredients in medium bowl. Spoon into decorative cellophane bag or airtight container. Place in basket.

Measure both amounts of raisins into separate cellophane bags. Place in basket.

Measure molasses into jar with tight-fitting lid. Place in basket. Wrap basket with cellophane and tie with ribbon. Makes 1 mix.

Pictured on page 53.

Directions for Boston Brown Loaves:

Soak clay pots in water for 30 minutes. Line bottom of each pot with waxed paper. Place on baking sheet. Empty cornmeal mixture into large bowl. Make a well in centre. Set aside. Combine raisins and molasses in medium bowl. Add 1 3/4 cups (425 mL) buttermilk and 1 tsp. (5 mL) apple cider (or white) vinegar. Stir. Add to well. Stir until just moistened. Divide and spoon batter into clay pots. Bake in 350ºF (175ºC) oven for 30 to 35 minutes until wooden pick inserted in centre of loaf comes out clean. Let stand in pots for 10 minutes before removing to wire racks to cool. Makes 7 loaves. Each loaf cuts into 3 slices, for a total of 21 slices.

1 slice: 131 Calories; 0.6 g Total Fat (0.1 g Mono, 0.2 g Poly, 0.2 g Sat); 1 mg Cholesterol; 30 g Carbohydrate; 2 g Fibre; 3 g Protein; 202 mg Sodium

Tomato Basil Seasoning

Strong basil and mild tomato flavours blend well in this great little gift that's always in season! Clean, sterile baby food jars are perfect to fill with this savoury mixture and tuck into a stocking or gift basket.

Dried basil	2 tbsp.	30 mL
Garlic powder	2 tbsp.	30 mL
Dry tomato basil soup mix, stir before measuring	1 tbsp.	15 mL
Onion powder	1 tbsp.	15 mL
Parsley flakes	1 tbsp.	15 mL
Dried whole oregano	1 tbsp.	15 mL
Dried thyme	1 tbsp.	15 mL
Dried marjoram	1 tsp.	5 mL

Measure all 8 ingredients into small bowl. Stir well. Spoon into jar with tight-fitting lid. Makes about 2/3 cup (150 mL).

1/2 tsp. (2 mL): 3 Calories; 0 g Total Fat (0 g Mono, 0 g Poly, 0 g Sat); 0 mg Cholesterol; 1 g Carbohydrate; trace Fibre; 0 g Protein; 6 mg Sodium

Pictured on page 54 and on back cover.

Directions for Tomato Basil Seasoning:

Sprinkle over beef, pork, poultry or white fish. Let stand for at least 30 minutes before cooking. For best flavour, sprinkle over meat, poultry or fish and chill for 4 hours before cooking.

Directions for Tomato Basil Vinaigrette:

Measure 3 tbsp. (50 mL) olive (or cooking) oil, 2 tbsp. (30 mL) red wine vinegar, 2 tsp. (10 mL) Tomato Basil Seasoning and 1 tsp. (5 mL) granulated sugar into jar with tight-fitting lid. Shake well. Drizzle over your favourite greens. Makes about 1/3 cup (75 mL).

2 tsp. (10 mL): 47 Calories; 5 g Total Fat (3.7 g Mono, 0.4 g Poly, 0.7 g Sat); 0 mg Cholesterol; 1 g Carbohydrate; trace Fibre; 0 g Protein; 3 mg Sodium

Left: Calico Bean Soup Mix, page 52

Right: Boston Brown Loaves Mix, page 52

Measure all 8 ingredients into small bowl. Stir well. Spoon into jar with tight-fitting lid. Makes about 1/2 cup (125 mL).

1/2 tsp. (2 mL): 3 Calories; 0.1 g Total Fat (0 g Mono, 0 g Poly, 0 g Sat); 0 mg Cholesterol; 1 g Carbohydrate; trace Fibre; 0 g Protein; 1 mg Sodium

Pictured on this page and on back cover.

Directions for Special Curry Rub:

Rub on beef, pork or poultry. Let stand for at least 30 minutes before cooking. For best flavour, rub on meat or poultry and chill for 4 hours before cooking.

Cajun Seasoning

An excellent seasoning to spice things up! Use mortar and pestle or clean coffee bean grinder to crush fennel seed. Tie your favourite jambalaya recipe to the jar with a pretty ribbon for a great gift.

Paprika	1/4 cup	60 mL
Dried basil	3 tbsp.	50 mL
Minced onion flakes	2 tbsp.	30 mL
Garlic powder	2 tbsp.	30 mL
Fennel seed, crushed	1 tbsp.	15 mL
Parsley flakes	1 tbsp.	15 mL
Dried thyme	2 tsp.	10 mL
Cayenne pepper	1 1/2 tsp.	7 mL
Salt	1 tbsp.	15 mL
Pepper	1 tsp.	5 mL

Measure all 10 ingredients into small bowl. Stir well. Spoon into jar with tight-fitting lid. Makes about 1 cup (250 mL).

1/2 tsp. (2 mL): 3 Calories; 0.1 g Total Fat (0 g Mono, 0 g Poly, 0 g Sat); 0 mg Cholesterol; 1 g Carbohydrate; trace Fibre; 0 g Protein; 94 mg Sodium

Pictured on this page and on back cover.

Directions for Cajun Seasoning:

Sprinkle over poultry, fish or shrimp. Let stand for at least 30 minutes before cooking. For best flavour, sprinkle over poultry, fish or shrimp and chill for 4 hours before cooking.

Top: Cajun Seasoning, this page
Centre: Special Curry Rub, below
Bottom: Tomato Basil Seasoning, page 53

Special Curry Rub

A mild, fragrant blend to use in place of store-bought curry powder. Give in a trio of spice mixes, with Tomato Basil Seasoning, page 53, and Cajun Seasoning, this page.

Ground coriander	3 tbsp.	50 mL
Ground cumin	2 tbsp.	30 mL
Turmeric	1 tbsp.	15 mL
Ground ginger	2 tsp.	10 mL
Ground cinnamon	1 tsp.	5 mL
Chili powder	1 tsp.	5 mL
Pepper	1/2 tsp.	1 mL
Ground cloves	1/4 tsp.	2 mL

Centre: Curried Lentil Soup Mix, below

Right: Seeded Flatbread Sticks, page 105

Curried Lentil Soup Mix

Assemble soup mix ingredients in a tall, narrow jar to best display layers. Makes a great gift basket duo with Seeded Flatbread Sticks, page 105.

Curry powder	1 tbsp.	15 mL
Chicken bouillon powder	2 tbsp.	30 mL
Onion flakes	2 tbsp.	30 mL
Dried mint leaves	1 tbsp.	15 mL
Garlic powder	2 tsp.	10 mL
Ground ginger	1 tsp.	5 mL
Dried red split lentils	1/4 cup	60 mL
Dried green lentils	3/4 cup	175 mL
Long grain brown rice	1/2 cup	125 mL

Layer all 9 ingredients, in order given, in jar with tight-fitting lid. Makes about 2 cups (500 mL).

Pictured above.

Directions for Curried Lentil Soup:

Combine contents of jar, 8 cups (2 L) water and 28 oz. (796 mL) can of diced tomatoes (with juice) in large pot or Dutch oven. Bring to a boil on medium-high. Reduce heat to medium-low. Cover. Simmer for 45 to 50 minutes, stirring occasionally, until lentils and rice are tender. Makes about 11 cups (2.75 L).

1 cup (250 mL): 123 Calories; 1 g Total Fat (0.3 g Mono, 0.3 g Poly, 0.2 g Sat); 0 mg Cholesterol; 23 g Carbohydrate; 3 g Fibre; 7 g Protein; 478 mg Sodium

Rosemary Lemon Rub

Lemon and mint add a refreshing aroma to this versatile mixture. A must-have for every pantry. The Barbecue gift basket on page 180 isn't complete without it.

Brown sugar, packed	2 tbsp.	30 mL
Lemon pepper	1 tbsp.	15 mL
Dried rosemary, crushed	1 tbsp.	15 mL
Dried mint leaves	1 tbsp.	15 mL
Ground cumin	2 tsp.	10 mL
Chili powder	1 tsp.	5 mL
Salt	1/2 tsp.	2 mL
Pepper	1/2 tsp.	2 mL

Measure all 8 ingredients into small bowl. Stir well. Spoon into jar with tight-fitting lid. Makes about 1/3 cup (75 mL).

1/2 tsp. (2 mL): 5 Calories; 0.1 g Total Fat (0 g Mono, 0 g Poly, 0 g Sat); 0 mg Cholesterol; 1 g Carbohydrate; trace Fibre; 0 g Protein; 144 mg Sodium

Pictured below and on page 180.

Directions for Rosemary Lemon Rub:

Rub on beef, lamb or poultry. Let stand for at least 30 minutes before cooking. For best flavour, rub on meat or poultry and chill for 4 hours before cooking.

Barbecue Seasoning

A handy mix to have at the ready—a welcome gift for any cook! Pair with Rosemary Lemon Rub in a Barbecue gift basket, page 180.

Paprika	1/4 cup	60 mL
Garlic powder	2 tbsp.	30 mL
Parsley flakes	2 tbsp.	30 mL
Granulated sugar	1 tbsp.	15 mL
Ground cinnamon	1 tsp.	5 mL
Ground ginger	1 tsp.	5 mL
Salt	2 tbsp.	30 mL
Pepper	1 tsp.	5 mL

Measure all 8 ingredients into small bowl. Stir well. Spoon into jar with tight-fitting lid. Makes about 3/4 cup (175 mL).

1/2 tsp. (2 mL): 3 Calories; 0.1 g Total Fat (0 g Mono, 0 g Poly, 0 g Sat); 0 mg Cholesterol; 1 g Carbohydrate; trace Fibre; 0 g Protein; 188 mg Sodium

Pictured below and on page 180.

Directions for Barbecue Seasoning:

Sprinkle over beef, pork, poultry or fish. Let stand for at least 30 minutes before cooking. For best flavour, sprinkle over meat, poultry or fish and chill for 4 hours before cooking.

Left: Rosemary Lemon Rub, above
Centre: Barbecue Seasoning, above

Bottom Centre: Nacho Shake, below
Centre: Parmesan Dill Popcorn, this page

Top Right: Nacho Popcorn, this page
Bottom Right: Parmesan Dill Shake, below

Nacho Shake

That's right—it's not for you! Put it in a festive tin with a jar of Parmesan Dill Shake and a cellophane bag of unpopped popcorn.

Grated Parmesan cheese	1/2 cup	125 mL
Paprika	1 tsp.	5 mL
Chili powder	1 tsp.	5 mL
Ground cumin	1/2 tsp.	2 mL
Cayenne pepper	1/4 tsp.	1 mL
Pepper	1/4 tsp.	1 mL

Measure all 6 ingredients into small bowl. Stir well. Spoon into jar with tight-fitting lid. Store in refrigerator for up to 2 months. Makes about 1/2 cup (125 mL).

1 tsp. (5 mL): 10 Calories; 0.7 g Total Fat (0.2 g Mono, 0 g Poly, 0.4 g Sat); 2 mg Cholesterol; 0 g Carbohydrate; trace Fibre; 1 g Protein; 41 mg Sodium

Pictured above and on page 177.

Directions for Nacho Popcorn:

Sprinkle over hot buttered popcorn. Toss well.

Parmesan Dill Shake

A great gift for the holiday season. Give it to your favourite snacker along with a jar of Nacho Shake in a Snack Attack gift basket, page 177, to sprinkle over popcorn for a nice change from chips.

Grated Parmesan cheese	1 cup	250 mL
Dill weed	1 1/2 tbsp.	25 mL
Garlic salt	1 tsp.	5 mL

Measure all 3 ingredients into small bowl. Stir well. Spoon into jar with tight-fitting lid. Store in refrigerator for up to 2 months. Makes about 1 cup (250 mL).

1 tsp. (5 mL): 10 Calories; 0.6 g Total Fat (0.2 g Mono, 0 g Poly, 0.4 g Sat); 2 mg Cholesterol; 0 g Carbohydrate; 0 g Fibre; 1 g Protein; 63 mg Sodium

Pictured above and on page 177.

Directions for Parmesan Dill Popcorn:

Sprinkle over hot buttered popcorn. Toss well.

Blondie Square Mix

Rich, sweet and chewy—the perfect square!
Package in a tall jar and top with a festive stocking cap!

Brown sugar, packed	1 1/2 cups	375 mL
All-purpose flour	2 cups	500 mL
Baking powder	1/2 tsp.	2 mL
Salt	1/8 tsp.	0.5 mL
Chopped pecans	1 1/2 cups	375 mL
Medium unsweetened coconut	1 1/2 cups	375 mL
Golden raisins	1 cup	250 mL

Pack brown sugar into jar with tight-fitting lid.

Combine flour, baking powder and salt in small bowl. Spoon on top of brown sugar in jar.

Layer remaining 3 ingredients, in order given, on top of flour mixture in jar. Makes about 6 1/2 cups (1.6 L).

Pictured on page 59.

Directions for Blondie Squares:

Beat 1/2 cup (125 mL) softened hard margarine (or butter), 3 large eggs and 1 tsp. (5 mL) almond flavouring in extra-large bowl until smooth. Mixture may look curdled. Add contents of jar. Mix well. Spread evenly in greased 9 × 9 inch (22 × 22 cm) pan. Bake in 350°F (175°C) oven for 30 to 35 minutes until golden and wooden pick inserted in centre comes out clean. Cool. Cuts into 16 squares.

1 square: 375 Calories; 20.8 g Total Fat (9.5 g Mono, 2.8 g Poly, 7.3 g Sat); 40 mg Cholesterol; 46 g Carbohydrate; 2 g Fibre; 5 g Protein; 127 mg Sodium

---

Pictured on page 59.

Rainbow Drop Cookie Mix

Peanut butter and chocolate chip cookies. Does it get any better? A great gift for that up-and-coming baker you know—add an apron and a wooden spoon, just for fun!

Granulated sugar	1/4 cup	60 mL
Brown sugar, packed	1/2 cup	125 mL
All-purpose flour	1 1/2 cups	375 mL
Baking soda	3/4 tsp.	4 mL
Baking powder	1/4 tsp.	1 mL
Mini candy-coated chocolates (such as mini M & M's)	1/2 cup	125 mL
Quick-cooking rolled oats (not instant)	1/2 cup	125 mL
Peanut butter chips	1/2 cup	125 mL
Crisp rice cereal	1/2 cup	125 mL

Layer both sugars, in order given, in jar with tight-fitting lid.

Combine flour, baking soda and baking powder in small bowl. Spoon on top of brown sugar in jar.

Layer remaining 4 ingredients, in order given, on top of flour mixture in jar. Makes about 3 3/4 cups (925 mL).

Pictured on page 59.

Directions for Rainbow Drop Cookies:

Beat 1/2 cup (125 mL) softened hard margarine (or butter), 2 large eggs and 1/2 tsp. (2 mL) vanilla in large bowl until smooth. Mixture may look curdled. Add contents of jar. Mix well. Drop, using 2 tsp. (10 mL) for each, about 2 inches (5 cm) apart onto ungreased cookie sheets. Bake in 350°F (175°C) oven for about 10 minutes until golden. Let stand on cookie sheets for 5 minutes before removing to wire racks to cool. Makes 4 1/2 dozen (54) cookies.

1 cookie: 69 Calories; 3.2 g Total Fat (1.5 g Mono, 0.3 g Poly, 0.8 g Sat); 9 mg Cholesterol; 9 g Carbohydrate; trace Fibre; 1 g Protein; 55 mg Sodium

---

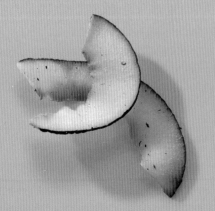

Top Left: Blondie Square Mix, this page
Right: Rainbow Drop Cookie Mix, above
Bottom Left: Blondie Squares, this page

Mango Spice Muffin Mix

Delicately flavoured, with just enough spice to fill the kitchen with a warm, inviting aroma. A scrumptious mix to put in a Tea Break gift basket, page 179.

All-purpose flour	2 1/2 cups	625 mL
Chopped dried mango	1 cup	250 mL
Brown sugar, packed	2/3 cup	150 mL
Whole wheat flour	1/2 cup	125 mL
Skim milk powder	1/2 cup	125 mL
Baking powder	4 tsp.	20 mL
Ground cinnamon	2 tsp.	10 mL
Ground nutmeg	1/2 tsp.	2 mL
Salt	1 tsp.	5 mL

Combine all 9 ingredients in large bowl. Spoon into decorative cellophane bag. Makes about 4 cups (1 L).

Pictured on page 61 and on page 179.

Directions for Mango Spice Muffins:

Measure 2 cups (500 mL) Mango Spice Muffin Mix into large bowl. Make a well in centre. Beat 1 large egg with fork in small bowl. Add 3/4 cup (175 mL) orange juice and 1/4 cup (60 mL) cooking oil. Stir. Add to well. Stir until just moistened. Grease 12 muffin cups with cooking spray. Fill cups 1/2 full. Bake in 400°F (205°C) oven for 10 to 12 minutes until wooden pick inserted in centre of muffin comes out clean. Let stand in pan for 5 minutes before removing to wire rack to cool. Makes 12 small muffins.

1 muffin: 169 Calories; 5.6 g Total Fat (3.1 g Mono, 1.6 g Poly, 0.6 g Sat); 18 mg Cholesterol; 27 g Carbohydrate; 1 g Fibre; 4 g Protein; 184 mg Sodium

---

Pictured on page 61.

Top Left: Cranberry Chip Cookie Mix, page 62
Top Centre: Raisin Pecan Square Mix, page 62
Right: Mango Spice Muffin Mix, this page
Bottom Centre: Mango Spice Muffins, above
Bottom Left: Cranberry Chip Cookies, page 62

Raisin Pecan Square Mix

*A simple mix to make—even simpler to bake!
Present with a can of sweetened condensed milk,
a festive oven mitt and apron set, and a shiny
new pan to delight a baker's heart.*

Medium unsweetened coconut	1 cup	250 mL
Milk chocolate chips	1 cup	250 mL
Golden raisins	1 1/4 cups	300 mL
Pecan pieces, toasted (see Tip, page 22), see Note	1 1/2 cups	375 mL

Layer all 4 ingredients, in order given, in decorative jar with tight-fitting lid. Makes about 4 1/2 cups (1.1 L).

Pictured on page 61.

Note: Cool pecans completely before adding to jar.

Directions for Raisin Pecan Squares:

Empty contents of jar into medium bowl. Stir well. Spread evenly in greased foil-lined 9 × 13 inch (22 × 33 cm) pan. Drizzle 11 oz. (300 mL) can of sweetened condensed milk evenly over pecan mixture. Do not stir. Bake in 375°F (190°C) oven for about 15 minutes until bubbling. Reduce heat to 350°F (175°C). Bake for 10 to 12 minutes until golden. Cool. Cuts into 24 squares.

1 square: 188 Calories; 11.1 g Total Fat (4.3 g Mono, 1.4 g Poly, 4.9 g Sat); 7 mg Cholesterol; 22 g Carbohydrate; 1 g Fibre; 3 g Protein; 29 mg Sodium

---

Cranberry Chip Cookie Mix

*White chocolate and flavourful cranberries
make a sweet gift!*

All-purpose flour	1 3/4 cups	425 mL
Granulated sugar	1/2 cup	125 mL
Baking soda	1 tsp.	5 mL
Brown sugar, packed	1/2 cup	125 mL
White chocolate chips	1 cup	250 mL
Dried cranberries	1/2 cup	125 mL

Combine flour, granulated sugar and baking soda in small bowl. Spoon into jar with tight-fitting lid.

Layer remaining 3 ingredients, in order given, on top of flour mixture in jar. Makes about 4 1/2 cups (1.1 L).

Pictured on page 40 and on page 60.

Directions for Cranberry Chip Cookies:

Beat 1/3 cup (75 mL) softened hard margarine (or butter), 2 eggs and 1 tsp. (5 mL) vanilla in large bowl until smooth. Mixture may look curdled. Add contents of jar. Mix well. Drop, using 2 tsp. (10 mL) for each, about 1 inch (2.5 cm) apart onto greased cookie sheets. Bake in 375°F (190°C) oven for 6 to 8 minutes until golden. Let stand on cookie sheets for 5 minutes before removing to wire racks to cool. Makes 5 dozen (60) cookies.

1 cookie: 58 Calories; 2.2 g Total Fat (1.1 g Mono, 0.2 g Poly, 0.8 g Sat); 8 mg Cholesterol; 9 g Carbohydrate; trace Fibre; 1 g Protein; 40 mg Sodium

---

Top Right: Blueberry Pancake Mix, page 64
Centre: Maple-Flavoured Syrup, page 79
Left: Blueberry Lime Syrup, page 79

Blueberry Pancake Mix

A wonderful hostess gift for making a quick breakfast for guests. Also great to take along when you're the out-of-town guest! Pair with Maple-Flavoured Syrup, page 79, or Blueberry Lime Syrup, page 79.

All-purpose flour	8 cups	2 L
Buttermilk powder	1 1/2 cups	375 mL
Baking powder	1/3 cup	75 mL
Granulated sugar	1/4 cup	60 mL
Salt	1 1/2 tsp.	7 mL
Cooking oil	3/4 cup	175 mL
Dried blueberries	1 cup	250 mL

Combine first 5 ingredients in large bowl.

Add cooking oil in thin stream while beating on low until mixture is crumbly.

Add blueberries. Toss well. Spoon into decorative airtight container. Makes about 12 cups (3 L).

Pictured on page 63.

Directions for Blueberry Pancakes:

Measure 3 cups (750 mL) Blueberry Pancake Mix into medium bowl. Make a well in centre. Beat 1 large egg with fork in small bowl. Add 1 1/2 cups (375 mL) water. Stir. Add to well. Stir until just mixed. Batter will be lumpy. Add more water if necessary until thick pouring consistency. Heat 1/2 tsp. (2 mL) cooking oil in large frying pan on medium until hot. Pour batter into pan, using about 1/4 cup (60 mL) for each pancake. Cook for 2 to 3 minutes until edges appear dry and bubbles form on top. Adjust heat if necessary. Turn pancakes. Cook for 1 to 2 minutes until golden. Remove to large plate. Cover to keep warm. Repeat with remaining batter, adding more cooking oil to pan if necessary to prevent sticking. Makes about 12 pancakes. Serves 4.

1 serving: 457 Calories; 15.9 g Total Fat (8.5 g Mono, 4.4 g Poly, 1.9 g Sat); 62 mg Cholesterol; 66 g Carbohydrate; 3 g Fibre; 13 g Protein; 688 mg Sodium

---

Chocolate Pudding Garden Mix

Package this sweet pudding mix with an assortment of garnishes individually wrapped in decorative cellophane bags for a gift kids will love! Or make some Easy Royal Icing "Bugs," page 66, to decorate your Chocolate Pudding Garden.

Brown sugar, packed	1 cup	250 mL
Skim milk powder	2/3 cup	150 mL
Cornstarch	1/2 cup	125 mL
Semi-sweet chocolate chips	1/4 cup	60 mL
Salt	1/4 tsp.	1 mL

GARDEN VARIETY GARNISHES
Chocolate wafer crumbs (dirt)
Gummy worms (worms)
Raisins (bugs and beetles)
Red licorice strings
   (red wigglers)
Speckled jelly beans (ladybugs
   and beetles)

Combine first 5 ingredients in medium bowl. Spoon into decorative cellophane bag or jar with tight-fitting lid. Makes about 2 1/3 cups (575 mL).

Pictured on page 65.

Directions for Chocolate Pudding:

Measure 1/2 of Chocolate Pudding Garden Mix into medium saucepan. Add 1 1/2 cups (375 mL) milk and 1 tsp. (5 mL) vanilla. Heat and stir on medium for 5 to 7 minutes until boiling and thickened. Let stand for 5 minutes to cool slightly. Spoon pudding into 4 serving bowls. Cool. Serves 4.

1 serving: 229 Calories; 2.2 g Total Fat (0.7 g Mono, 0.1 g Poly, 1.3 g Sat); 4 mg Cholesterol; 47 g Carbohydrate; trace Fibre; 6 g Protein; 170 mg Sodium

Directions for Chocolate Pudding Garden:

Create a unique garden dessert. Top pudding with chocolate crumbs and an assortment of "bug-like" garnishes, or make your own using Easy Royal Icing "Bugs," page 66.

Pictured on page 65.

Top: Chocolate Pudding Garden Mix, this page
Bottom: Chocolate Pudding Garden, above
Top and Bottom: Easy Royal Icing "Bugs,"
page 66

Easy Royal Icing "Bugs"

Use these squirmy, sweet treats to decorate the Chocolate Pudding Garden, page 64.

QUICK AND EASY ROYAL ICING

Icing (confectioner's) sugar	2 cups	500 mL
Egg white (large)	1	1
Water	1 tbsp.	15 mL

Beat all 3 ingredients in small bowl for 1 to 2 minutes until stiff peaks form.

LADYBUGS

Black licorice nib, halved lengthwise	1
Red candy melting wafers, halved	2
Quick And Easy Royal Icing	

Take 1 nib half and lay flat. Shape one end to look like a head by using scissors to round corners.

Attach 2 candy wafer halves to nib half with icing to look like wings. Repeat with remaining nib half and wafer halves. Makes 2 ladybugs.

Pictured on page 65.

FLIES

Black licorice nib, halved lengthwise	1
Blue candy melting wafers, halved	2
Quick And Easy Royal Icing	

Follow instructions for ladybugs. Omit red candy melting wafers. Use blue candy wafers for wings. Makes 2 flies.

Pictured on page 65.

BUMBLEBEES

Black licorice nib, halved lengthwise	1
Yellow half-moon jujubes, halved crosswise	2
Quick And Easy Royal Icing	

Take 1 nib half and lay flat. Shape one end to look like a head by using scissors to round corners. Take 2 jujube halves and lay flat. Trim to make 2 wing shapes.

Attach jujube wings to nib half with icing. Repeat with remaining nib half and 2 jujube halves. Makes 2 bumblebees.

Pictured on page 65.

SNAILS

Miniature marshmallow	1
Half-moon jujube	1
Quick And Easy Royal Icing	
Black shoestring licorice (3/4 inch, 2 cm, length), halved	1

Squeeze 1 end of marshmallow between your fingers until flattened. Attach flattened marshmallow edge to flat side of jujube with icing.

Make 2 small holes in top of marshmallow with wooden pick where antennae will be. Put 1 shoestring licorice half into each hole. Makes 1 snail.

Pictured on page 65.

Dessert Pizza Mix

A great addition to the Kid's Best Friend gift basket, page 172. Or pair with a new mixing bowl and wooden spoon. They may even share dessert with you!

All-purpose flour	2 cups	500 mL
Granulated sugar	1 cup	250 mL
Baking powder	1 tsp.	5 mL
Salt	1/2 tsp.	2 mL
Semi-sweet chocolate chips	1 cup	250 mL
Peanut butter chips	1 cup	250 mL
Miniature multi-coloured marshmallows	1 cup	250 mL

Combine first 4 ingredients in medium bowl. Spoon into jar with tight-fitting lid.

Measure remaining 3 ingredients into separate decorative cellophane bags. Place on top of flour mixture in jar. Makes about 6 cups (1.5 L).

Pictured on this page and on page 173.

Directions for Dessert Pizza:

Remove bags from jar. Set aside. Beat 1/2 cup (125 mL) softened hard margarine (or butter), 2 large eggs and 1/2 tsp. (2 mL) vanilla in large bowl until smooth. Mixture may look curdled. Add contents of jar. Stir until mixture resembles coarse crumbs. Shape dough into ball. Press in greased 12 inch (30 cm) pizza pan, forming rim around edge. Bake in 350°F (175°C) oven for about 15 minutes until edge is golden. Remove from oven. Sprinkle chocolate chips, peanut butter chips and marshmallows over top. Bake for about 5 minutes until chips start to melt. Cool. Cuts into 12 wedges.

1 wedge: 412 Calories; 19.7 g Total Fat (8.9 g Mono, 1.9 g Poly, 7.3 g Sat); 38 mg Cholesterol; 57 g Carbohydrate; 2 g Fibre; 6 g Protein; 295 mg Sodium

Gingerbread Cookie Mix

Include a variety bag of small candies for the recipient to use to decorate these sweet, spicy cookies. Be sure to label the jars containing the cookie mix and the icing mix. A great parent-and-kids project.

GINGERBREAD COOKIE MIX

Brown sugar, packed	1 cup	250 mL
All-purpose flour	1 1/3 cups	325 mL
Baking powder	3/4 tsp.	4 mL
Baking soda	3/4 tsp.	4 mL
All-purpose flour	1 1/3 cups	325 mL
Ground ginger	1 1/2 tsp.	7 mL
Ground cloves	3/4 tsp.	4 mL
Ground cinnamon	3/4 tsp.	4 mL
Ground allspice	3/4 tsp.	4 mL

ICING MIX

Icing (confectioner's) sugar	2 2/3 cups	650 mL
Meringue powder (see Note)	2 tbsp.	30 mL

Gingerbread Cookie Mix: Pack brown sugar in even layer into jar with tight-fitting lid.

Combine first amount of flour, baking powder and baking soda in small bowl. Spoon on top of brown sugar in jar. Pack down gently.

Combine next 5 ingredients in same small bowl. Spoon on top of flour mixture in jar. Makes about 3 cups (750 mL) mix.

Icing Mix: Combine icing sugar and meringue powder in small bowl. Spoon into decorative cellophane bag or separate jar with tight-fitting lid. Makes about 2 3/4 cups (675 mL).

Pictured on page 69.

Note: Meringue powder can be purchased at specialty kitchen stores or where cake decorating supplies are sold.

Directions for Gingerbread Cookies:

Beat 1/2 cup (125 mL) fancy (mild) molasses, 1/3 cup (75 mL) softened hard margarine (or butter) and 1 large egg in large bowl until smooth. Mixture may look curdled. Add Gingerbread Cookie Mix. Mix well. Dough will be stiff. Divide dough in half. Shape each half into ball. Flatten each ball into disc and wrap with plastic wrap. Chill for 30 minutes.

Discard plastic wrap from 1 disc. Roll out dough on lightly floured surface to about 1/4 inch (6 mm) thickness. Cut out shapes with lightly floured 2 inch (5 cm) cookie cutters. Roll out scraps to cut more shapes. Arrange 2 inches (5 cm) apart on greased cookie sheets. Bake in 350ºF (175ºC) oven for 8 to 10 minutes until firm. Let stand on cookie sheets for 5 minutes before removing to wire racks to cool. Cool cookie sheets between batches. Repeat with remaining disc.

Icing: Beat Icing Mix and 1/4 cup (60 mL) cold water in large bowl until stiff peaks form. Add more water, 1/2 tsp. (2 mL) at a time, if necessary until piping consistency. Divide icing among several small bowls. Colour as desired with various paste food colourings. Spoon each colour of icing into separate paper cones (page 27), or into separate small resealable freezer bags with tiny piece snipped off corner. Pipe icing onto cookies as desired. Makes about 40 cookies.

1 cookie: 116 Calories; 1.8 g Total Fat (1.1 g Mono, 0.2 g Poly, 0.4 g Sat); 5 mg Cholesterol; 24 g Carbohydrate; trace Fibre; 1 g Protein; 60 mg Sodium

Pictured on page 69.

Left: Gingerbread Cookie Mix, this page
Top and Bottom Right: Gingerbread Cookies, above

Gifts for the Home

This charming potpourri of gift ideas offers sensational scents, soothing bath bags, fragrant oils and gifts for the home. Create a spicy trivet or a festive centrepiece to bring good tidings to those you love. And remember the beloved family dog or cat with a gift bag of tempting biscuits. Feature one or more of these special gifts as you create your own themed gift basket—both the gift and the effort will be appreciated.

Cinnamon Citrus Potpourri

An aromatic mixture for the home. Fill cellophane bags and tie with raffia for a great hostess or teacher gift. Or put it in a fancy bowl topped with a festive ribbon.

Red medium apples (with peel)	2	2
Lemon juice	1 tbsp.	15 mL
Medium oranges (see Note)	4	4
Medium lemons (see Note)	4	4
Cinnamon sticks (4 inches, 10 cm, each)	16	16
Whole cloves (see Tip, below)	2 cups	500 mL
Pure essential cinnamon oil (see Note)	1/4 tsp.	1 mL

Slice apples crosswise through cores into 1/4 inch (6 mm) slices. Brush both sides of each slice with lemon juice. Arrange in single layer on greased baking sheets. Bake in 200ºF (95ºC) oven for 2 1/2 to 3 hours, depending on moisture content of apples, turning slices once each hour until dried. Immediately transfer to wire racks to cool. Put into extra-large bowl.

Slice oranges and lemons crosswise into 1/4 inch (6 mm) slices. Arrange in single layer on greased baking sheets. Bake in 200ºF (95ºC) oven for 2 1/2 to 3 hours, depending on moisture content of fruit, turning slices once each hour until dried. Immediately transfer to wire racks to cool. Add to apple slices.

Add cinnamon sticks and cloves. Toss gently.

Drizzle with cinnamon oil. Toss gently. Store in airtight containers. Makes about 12 cups (3 L).

Pictured on page 70.

Note: For best results, use oranges and lemons with thin peel.

Note: Essential oils can be found in the fragrance section of drug stores or in craft stores.

Tip: Whole cloves can be very expensive when purchased in small bottles. The ethnic or bulk food section of your grocery store may provide a less expensive alternative.

Cloved Oranges

Hang these clove-covered oranges in any room and their spicy scent will fill it with a delightful holiday ambiance. Start to make these about 4 to 5 weeks ahead. Hang on the Christmas tree or place in a decorative bowl for an aromatic centrepiece.

Small oranges (see Note)	2	2
Bamboo or metal skewer		
Whole cloves, approximately (see Tip, this page)	1 oz.	30 g
Ground cinnamon	1 tsp.	5 mL
Ground nutmeg	1 tsp.	5 mL
Ground allspice	1 tsp.	5 mL
Ribbon (1/4 to 1/2 inch, 6 to 12 mm, width)		
Masking tape (1/4 to 1/2 inch, 6 to 12 mm, width)		

Measure circumference of each orange. Cut 3 strips of masking tape (same width as ribbon) the length of the circumference of each orange, for a total of 6 strips. Wrap 3 strips around each orange to divide into wedges.

Poke holes randomly, but close together, with skewer into untaped peel of both oranges. Push cloves into holes until untaped peel is completely covered.

Combine cinnamon, nutmeg and allspice in large resealable freezer bag. Place 1 orange in bag. Seal bag. Toss gently until coated. Transfer to wire rack set in baking sheet with sides. Repeat with remaining orange and spice mixture. Let stand on wire rack in cool, dry place for 4 to 5 weeks, gently tossing oranges in spice mixture once each week during drying time, until oranges harden.

Remove masking tape. Tie 3 ribbons in place of the masking tape around each orange. Tie loop with ribbon at top of each orange for hanging. To refresh fragrance, remove ribbon and shake oranges in resealable plastic bag with additional spice mixture. Replace ribbon. Makes 2 cloved oranges.

Pictured on page 72.

Note: Use freshly purchased oranges for best results. Oranges that have been in the refrigerator for awhile could mold before completely drying.

Cloved Oranges, page 71

Caramel Cinnamon Stir Sticks

Sweet caramel glistens on the ends of spicy cinnamon sticks.
Wrap individually in cellophane or tie a bunch together
with raffia or ribbon and nestle in a gift basket
of cider mixes, teas and coffees.

CARAMEL		
Granulated sugar	2 cups	500 mL
Water	1 cup	250 mL
Ice cubes		
Cold water		
Cinnamon sticks (4 inches, 10 cm, each)	36	36

Caramel: Heat and stir sugar and first amount of water in heavy medium saucepan on medium-low until sugar is dissolved. Bring to a boil on medium-high. Boil, uncovered, for 5 to 10 minutes without stirring, brushing side of saucepan with wet pastry brush to dissolve any sugar crystals, until golden brown. Pour into 2 cup (500 mL) heatproof liquid measure. Let stand for about 10 minutes, stirring twice, until starting to thicken. Makes about 1 1/4 cups (300 mL) caramel.

Put ice cubes into large glass. Fill with cold water. Set aside.

Holding 1 cinnamon stick by end, dip straight down into caramel until halfway up stick. Swirl stick in caramel to thickly coat (see Note). Immediately dip caramel-coated end of stick into ice water. Hold in water for 10 to 15 seconds until caramel is firm (see Note). Blot on tea towel to remove excess water. Place on parchment paper-lined baking sheet. Repeat with remaining cinnamon sticks, caramel and ice water. Let stand on baking sheet for about 48 hours, turning sticks occasionally, until caramel is hard. Store in airtight container for up to 1 month. Makes 36 stir sticks.

Pictured on page 43.

Note: If caramel becomes too thick for dipping, microwave on low (10%) for about 10 seconds to soften.

Note: Add more ice cubes as needed to keep water very cold.

Spice Trivet, page 73

Spice Trivet

This easy project can be sewn by machine or by hand. Placing a hot pot of tea or a hot casserole dish on top of this handy trivet will protect your table or countertop while creating a spicy, seasonal aroma. Tuck the trivet into a Tea Break gift basket, page 179, or give it to someone special along with a new teapot filled with assorted teas.

SPICE STUFFING

Cinnamon sticks (4 inches, 10 cm, each)	6	6
Whole cloves (see Tip, page 71)	2 tbsp.	30 mL
Whole allspice	2 tbsp.	30 mL
Dried lentils (or split peas)	1/2 cup	125 mL
Dried orange peel (see Note)	3 tbsp.	50 mL
Pure essential cinnamon oil (see Note)	1/4 tsp.	1 mL

MATERIALS Trivet Insert
2 insulated heatproof fabric squares (7 inches, 18 cm, each)

MATERIALS Decorative Cover
Cotton fabric rectangle (10 x 23 inches, 25 x 58 cm)

TOOLS
scissors, measuring tape, iron, pinking shears

Spice Stuffing: Put cinnamon sticks, cloves and allspice into large resealable freezer bag. Seal bag. Hit with meat mallet or hammer to crush spices. Add lentils and orange peel. Seal bag. Toss well. Drizzle with cinnamon oil. Seal bag. Toss well.

Note: Omit dried orange peel. Use same amount of dried zest. To make dried zest, spread zest from several oranges in greased shallow pan. Bake in 200ºF (95ºC) oven for about 15 minutes until dry. Store any remaining dried zest in jar with tight-fitting lid.

Note: Essential oils can be found in the fragrance section of drug stores or in craft stores.

Trivet Insert: Position the 2 insulated heatproof squares on top of each other, wrong sides together. Align the edges evenly. Pin in place.

Sew 3 sides together, leaving a 1/2 inch (1.2 cm) seam allowance. Sew 2 seams, each 2 1/4 inches (6 cm) from opposite sides of the square (see line drawing).

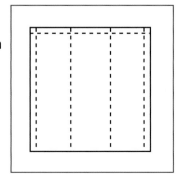

Divide and spoon the Spice Stuffing into each of the 3 pockets created. Sew the open end of the insert closed, leaving a 1/2 inch (1.2 cm) seam allowance.

Decorative Cover: Place the cotton fabric rectangle right-side down on the ironing board. Fold over a 1/2 inch (1.2 cm) hem on each short side. Iron the folded edges. Sew the hem in place.

Fold over 4 inches (10 cm) of the fabric towards the centre. Iron the folded edge (see line drawing). Fold the resulting rectangle in half, aligning the edges, to form a square pocket. Pin the sides in place.

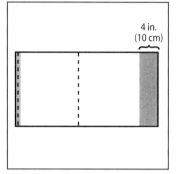

4 in. (10 cm)

Sew the sides together, leaving a 1/2 inch (1.2 cm) seam allowance. With pinking shears, cut a decorative edge along the 2 seam allowances of the square pocket.

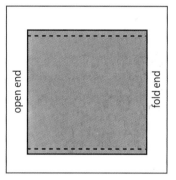

open end

fold end

Put the trivet insert into the square pocket, fitting it into the corners and tucking one end under the 4 inch (10 cm) fold. The cover may be removed for cleaning.

Pictured on page 72 and on page 179.

Lavender Massage Oil

Give this to someone special in a Stress Buster gift basket, page 179, along with Lavender Milk Bath Bags, this page.

Safflower oil	1 1/2 cups	375 mL
Almond oil	1 cup	250 mL
Drops of pure essential lavender oil (see Note)	30	30
Drops of pure essential rosemary oil (see Note)	20	20
Sprigs of dried lavender, for decoration		

Combine first 4 ingredients in jar with tight-fitting lid. Shake well. Pour through funnel into decorative bottles with tight-fitting lids.

Put 1 lavender sprig into each bottle and label. Store in cool dry place for 3 to 4 months. Makes about 2 1/2 cups (625 mL).

Pictured on page 178.

Lavender Milk Bath Bags

A soothing, fragrant gift. Attach a tag with these instructions: Hold one of these bags under running water as you draw your bath, then leave it in the tub. Enjoy!

Skim milk powder	1 cup	250 mL
Dried lavender (or lavender flowers)	1 cup	250 mL
Quick-cooking rolled oats (not instant)	1/2 cup	125 mL
Drops of pure essential lavender oil (see Note)	20	20
Organza squares (9 inches, 22 cm, each)	20	20
Ribbon		

Combine first 4 ingredients in medium bowl. Makes about 2 1/2 cups (625 mL). Place 1 organza square on work surface. Lay second square on top diagonally to form diamond shape. Measure 1/4 cup (60 mL) milk bath into centre of diamond. Draw up corners and tie with ribbon. Repeat with remaining organza squares, milk bath and ribbon. Store in cool dry place for 3 to 4 months. Makes 10 bath bags.

Pictured on page 178.

Note: Essential oils can be found in the fragrance section of drug stores or in craft stores.

Doggy Delights

With a pat on his back, give Fido a snack—a tasty doggy bone.

Quick-cooking rolled oats (not instant)	1/2 cup	125 mL
Wheat germ	1/2 cup	125 mL
Instant soy drink powder	1/4 cup	60 mL
Brewer's yeast	2 tbsp.	30 mL
Low-sodium beef bouillon powder	1 tsp.	5 mL
Jars of strained beef baby food (3 1/2 oz., 100 mL, each)	2	2

Combine first 5 ingredients in medium bowl.

Add baby food. Mix well. Let stand for 1 hour. Turn out onto lightly floured surface. Roll or pat out to 1/2 inch (12 mm) thick rectangle. Cut out shapes with bone-shaped cookie cutter. Roll out scraps to cut more bones. Arrange about 2 inches (5 cm) apart on greased baking sheets. Bake in 300°F (150°C) oven for about 1 1/2 hours until hard and dry. Cool. Store in airtight container for up to 10 weeks. Makes about 1 1/2 dozen (18) treats.

Pictured on page 75.

Kitty Nibbles

Even though they pretend not to notice, the cats in your life won't be able to resist these tasty nibbles!

Wheat germ	1/4 cup	60 mL
Whole wheat flour	1/4 cup	60 mL
Instant soy drink powder	1/4 cup	60 mL
Brewer's yeast	1/4 cup	60 mL
Can of sardines in spring water (with liquid), mashed	3 1/4 oz.	106 g
Water	3 tbsp.	50 mL

Combine first 4 ingredients in medium bowl.

Add sardines with liquid and water. Mix well. Divide into 8 equal portions. Roll out each portion to 1/4 inch (6 mm) diameter rope. Cut into 1/4 inch (6 mm) pieces. Arrange evenly spaced apart on greased baking sheet. Flatten each piece slightly. Bake in 350°F (175°C) oven for about 8 minutes until hard and dry. Cool. Store in airtight container for up to 10 weeks. Makes about 3 cups (750 mL).

Pictured on page 75.

Horse Cookie Treats

To all you cowpokes—horses deserve a holiday treat, too!

Whole wheat flour	1 1/2 cups	375 mL
Ground flax	1 cup	250 mL
Natural wheat bran	1 cup	250 mL
Grated peeled apple, packed	1 cup	250 mL
Blackstrap molasses	1/2 cup	125 mL
Canola oil	1/4 cup	60 mL

Combine first 3 ingredients in large bowl. Add apple. Stir until coated.

Measure molasses and canola oil into medium bowl. Stir well. Add to apple mixture. Mix well. Shape into 2 inch (5 cm) diameter log. Wrap with waxed paper. Chill for 1 1/2 hours. Discard waxed paper. Cut log into 1/4 inch (6 mm) slices. Arrange about 2 inches (5 cm) apart on ungreased baking sheets. Bake in 325ºF (160ºC) oven for about 25 minutes until hard and dry. Cool. Store in airtight container for up to 10 weeks. Makes about 30 treats.

Pictured below.

Top: Horse Cookie Treats, above
Bottom Left: Kitty Nibbles, page 74
Bottom Right: Doggy Delights, page 74

Partridge In A Pear Tree

What would Christmas be without a partridge in a pear tree? This centrepiece will add a festive atmosphere to any room.

MATERIALS
Terra cotta pot (4 inch, 10 cm, diameter)
Gold spray paint
Dried florist foam
5 craft mini-pears
1/2 cup (125 mL) sanding (decorating) sugar (see Note)
Grapevine swag
Florist wire (22 gauge)
Mini-leaves craft pick
Craft bird (3 inch, 7.5 cm, size)
Star (2 inch, 5 cm, diameter)
Ribbon (1/2 inch, 12 mm, width), 33 inch (84 cm) length
Spanish moss

TOOLS
latex gloves, sharp knife, spray adhesive, needle-nose pliers, wire cutters, glue gun, scissors

Wearing latex gloves, spray the outside of the terra cotta pot with gold paint. Let dry completely. Trim the florist foam and fit inside the pot so the top of the foam is below the rim.

Holding 1 pear by the stem, spray adhesive to cover the pear. Immediately hold the pear over the sanding sugar in a small bowl and sprinkle with sugar until coated. Repeat with the remaining pears.

Select 4 thick, straight twigs from the grapevine swag to use for the tree trunk. Cut the twigs 14 inches (35 cm) long. Holding the twigs together, push them into the middle of the foam to the bottom of the pot. The twigs should extend about 10 inches (25 cm) above the pot rim.

To make the bottom cross branches, cut 4 thin twigs 11 inches (28 cm) long. Using the pliers, bind them together with florist wire. Centre the cross branches on the trunk about 3 inches (7.5 cm) above the pot rim. Using the pliers, attach the branches to the trunk with wire. Cut off any excess wire.

To make the middle cross branches, cut 4 thin twigs 8 inches (20 cm) long. Using the pliers, bind them together with wire and attach about 3 inches (7.5 cm) above the bottom branches. To make the top cross branches, cut 4 thin twigs 6 inches (15 cm) long. Using the pliers, bind them together with wire and attach about 3 inches (7.5 cm) above the middle branches.

Glue the leaves randomly onto the branches. Glue the pears to the branches, tucking the stems into the branches and leaves. Glue the bird to a branch, and the star to the top of the tree.

Glue the centre of the ribbon to the back of the pot on the rim. Wrap the ribbon around the rim and tie a bow in front. Trim the ends on an angle. Cover the foam with moss.

Pictured on page 77.

Note: Sanding sugar is a coarse decorating sugar that comes in white and various colours and is available at specialty kitchen stores.

Gifts in a Jar

There's no mystery to what's inside these gifts—a glass jar just can't keep a secret! This impressive collection of recipes offers the sweet, tangy and spicy flavours of tempting salsas, syrups, marinades, pesto and even liqueurs.

There are two ways in which these recipes are prepared: "processed" and "non-processed." Processed (or preserved) recipes have a longer shelf life and can be made earlier in the season when freshly grown produce is still available.

Non-processed recipes can be made up to four weeks in advance, but should be used within three weeks after giving. Don't forget to label your jars with "best-before" dates and storage instructions. And remember, preserved gifts should always be refrigerated after opening.

When all these gifts are prepared and ready for delivery, they'll still need your creative touch, so don't forget to dress up the lids with festive fabrics and ribbon.

Maple-Flavoured Syrup

This sweet syrup is great in a gift basket with Blueberry Pancake Mix, page 64. Demerara sugar gives it a dark colour and rich flavour.

Granulated sugar	3 cups	750 mL
Demerara (or brown) sugar, packed	2 cups	500 mL
Water	2 cups	500 mL
Salt, just a pinch		
Maple flavouring	1 tbsp.	15 mL

Heat and stir first 4 ingredients in large saucepan on medium-high for about 5 minutes until boiling and sugar is dissolved. Reduce heat to medium-low. Cover. Simmer for 10 minutes. Remove from heat. Let stand for 5 minutes.

Add flavouring. Stir well. Fill 4 hot sterile 1/2 pint (250 mL) jars to within 1/2 inch (12 mm) of top. Wipe rims. Place sterile metal lids on jars and screw on metal bands fingertip tight. Do not over-tighten. Process in boiling water bath for 5 minutes (see Note). Remove jars. Cool. Chill after opening. May be transferred to decorative bottle for gifting. Keep chilled. Makes about 4 cups (1 L).

1 tbsp. (15 mL): 63 Calories; 0 g Total Fat (0 g Mono, 0 g Poly, 0 g Sat); 0 mg Cholesterol; 16 g Carbohydrate; 0 g Fibre; 0 g Protein; 3 mg Sodium

Pictured on page 63.

Note: Processing time is for elevations 1001 to 3000 feet (306 to 915 m) above sea level. Make adjustment for elevation in your area if necessary.

Blueberry Lime Syrup

They'll have a blue, blueberry Christmas when they receive this tasty gift from your kitchen! Pour over pancakes or waffles for a sweet holiday brunch.

Bag of frozen blueberries	2 1/4 lbs.	1 kg
Granulated sugar	2 cups	500 mL
Orange-flavoured liqueur (such as Grand Marnier), or orange juice	1/4 cup	60 mL
Salt	1/4 tsp.	1 mL
Lime juice	3 – 4 tbsp.	50 – 60 mL

Combine first 4 ingredients in large pot or Dutch oven. Heat on medium-low for about 20 minutes, stirring occasionally, until sugar is dissolved. Bring to a boil on medium-high. Reduce heat to medium. Boil gently, uncovered, for 15 to 20 minutes, stirring occasionally, until slightly thickened. Mixture should lightly coat back of metal spoon. Press blueberry mixture through sieve into 4 cup (1 L) liquid measure. Discard solids.

Add lime juice. Stir well. Cool to room temperature. Pour into sterile jars or decorative bottles with tight-fitting lids. Store in refrigerator for up to 2 months. Makes about 3 3/4 cups (925 mL).

1 tbsp. (15 mL): 37 Calories; 0.1 g Total Fat (0 g Mono, 0 g Poly, 0 g Sat); 0 mg Cholesterol; 9 g Carbohydrate; 1 g Fibre; 0 g Protein; 10 mg Sodium

Pictured on page 63.

Roasted Peppers

A spicy part of the Italian gift basket, page 182. Or make your own gift basket that includes a jar of these colourful peppers. Chopped or sliced, these peppers are great on pasta, pizza or sandwiches.

Large red peppers, quartered, seeds and ribs removed	6	6
Large yellow peppers, quartered, seeds and ribs removed	6	6
Cooking (not olive) oil	1 cup	250 mL
Red wine vinegar	1/2 cup	125 mL
Salt	1 tsp.	5 mL
Yellow mustard seed	4 tsp.	20 mL
Dried crushed chilies	1 tsp.	5 mL
Dried rosemary, crushed	1 tsp.	5 mL

Arrange peppers in single layer, skin-side up, on ungreased baking sheets. Broil on top rack in oven for about 10 minutes until skins are blistered and blackened. Transfer to large bowl. Cover with plastic wrap. Let sweat for about 15 minutes until cool enough to handle. Remove skins. Cut each quarter in half lengthwise, for a total of 96 pieces.

Combine cooking oil, vinegar and salt in medium saucepan. Heat on medium for 5 to 10 minutes until very hot, but not boiling. Remove from heat.

Put 6 red and 6 yellow pepper pieces into each of 8 sterile 1/2 pint (250 mL) jars with tight-fitting lids. Measure 1/2 tsp. (2 mL) mustard seed, 1/8 tsp. (0.5 mL) chilies and 1/8 tsp. (0.5 mL) rosemary into each jar. Stir vinegar mixture. Spoon into each jar to within 1 inch (2.5 cm) of top. Cover with lids. Cool. Store in refrigerator for up to 1 month.

1 pepper piece: 18 Calories; 1.3 g Total Fat (0.7 g Mono, 0.4 g Poly, 0.1 g Sat); 0 mg Cholesterol; 2 g Carbohydrate; trace Fibre; 0 g Protein; 13 mg Sodium

Pictured on page 182.

Teriyaki Marinade

A mildly sweet 'n' tangy marinade that adds glistening appeal to grilled beef, chicken or pork skewers. A nice complement to the Barbecue gift basket, page 180.

White vinegar	1/3 cup	75 mL
Soy sauce	1/4 cup	60 mL
Liquid honey	3 tbsp.	50 mL
Dry white (or alcohol-free) wine	2 tbsp.	30 mL
Cooking oil	1 tbsp.	15 mL
Garlic cloves, minced (or 3/4 tsp., 4 mL, powder)	3	3
Finely grated, peeled gingerroot	1 tsp.	5 mL

Combine all 7 ingredients in 2 cup (500 mL) liquid measure. Pour into sterile jar or decorative bottle with tight-fitting lid. Store in refrigerator for up to 1 month. Makes about 1 cup (250 mL).

1 tbsp. (15 mL): 25 Calories; 0.8 g Total Fat (0.5 g Mono, 0.3 g Poly, 0.1 g Sat); 0 mg Cholesterol; 4 g Carbohydrate; trace Fibre; 0 g Protein; 264 mg Sodium

Pictured below and on page 180.

Directions for Teriyaki Marinade:

Place about 2 lbs. (900 g) cubed beef, chicken or pork in large resealable freezer bag. Pour marinade over top. Seal bag. Turn until coated. Marinate in refrigerator for at least 6 hours or overnight. Discard marinade. If preferred, drain marinade into small saucepan. Bring to a boil on medium. Reduce heat to medium-low and simmer, uncovered, for at least 5 minutes. Brush on meat while grilling.

Cran-Orange Chutney

A beautiful, ruby-red combination spiced to taste like Christmas. It's an excellent alternative to plain cranberry sauce to serve with the holiday turkey. Makes a thoughtful hostess gift.

Fresh (or frozen, thawed) cranberries	2 cups	500 mL
Cranberry cocktail	1/2 cup	125 mL
Medium oranges, peeled and coarsely chopped (about 1 cup, 250 mL)	2	2
Golden raisins	1/3 cup	75 mL
Chopped onion	1/4 cup	60 mL
Brown sugar, packed	1 cup	250 mL
Apple cider vinegar	1/2 cup	125 mL
Ground ginger	1/2 tsp.	2 mL
Ground cloves	1/2 tsp.	2 mL
Salt	1/2 tsp.	2 mL
Pepper	1/2 tsp.	2 mL
Ground cinnamon	1/4 tsp.	1 mL

Combine first 5 ingredients in large saucepan. Bring to a boil on medium-high. Reduce heat to medium-low. Simmer, uncovered, for about 2 minutes until cranberries are softened.

Add remaining 7 ingredients. Stir. Bring to a boil on medium. Reduce heat to medium-low. Simmer, uncovered, for 50 to 60 minutes, stirring occasionally, until slightly thickened. Remove from heat. Gently mash cranberries. Fill 5 hot sterile 1/2 cup (125 mL) jars to within 1/2 inch (12 mm) of top. Wipe rims. Place sterile metal lids on jars and screw on metal bands fingertip tight. Do not over-tighten. Process in boiling water bath for 15 minutes (see Note). Remove jars. Cool. Chill after opening. Makes about 2 1/2 cups (625 mL).

1 tbsp. (15 mL): 33 Calories; 0 g Total Fat (0 g Mono, 0 g Poly, 0 g Sat); 0 mg Cholesterol; 9 g Carbohydrate; trace Fibre; 0 g Protein; 31 mg Sodium

Pictured below.

Note: Processing time is for elevations 1001 to 3000 feet (306 to 915 m) above sea level. Make adjustment for elevation in your area if necessary.

Tapenade Salsa

Wish them a Joyeux Nöel with the delightful flavours of Provence mingled with traditional salsa ingredients. Great bundled with Wheat And Walnut Crackers, page 110. Even better—wrap it in a Snack Attack gift basket, page 177.

Can of sliced ripe olives, drained and chopped	4 1/2 oz.	125 mL
Chopped pimiento-stuffed olives (manzanilla olives)	1/2 cup	125 mL
Finely chopped red pepper	1/4 cup	60 mL
Finely chopped green pepper	1/4 cup	60 mL
Sun-dried tomatoes in oil, drained and finely chopped	1/4 cup	60 mL
Garlic clove, minced (or 1/4 tsp., 1 mL, powder)	1	1
Anchovy paste	1/2 tsp.	2 mL
Tomato juice	2 tbsp.	30 mL
Red wine vinegar	1 tbsp.	15 mL
Balsamic vinegar	1 tbsp.	15 mL
Lemon juice	1 tsp.	5 mL
Dried thyme	1/2 tsp.	2 mL
Dried whole oregano	1/2 tsp.	2 mL
Pepper	1/2 tsp.	2 mL

Combine first 7 ingredients in large bowl.

Measure remaining 7 ingredients into small saucepan. Heat and stir on medium for about 2 minutes until fragrant. Add to olive mixture. Stir well. Spoon into sterile jars with tight-fitting lids. Store in refrigerator for up to 1 week. Makes about 2 cups (500 mL).

1 tbsp. (15 mL): 8 Calories; 0.6 g Total Fat (0.4 g Mono, 0.1 g Poly, 0.1 g Sat); 0 mg Cholesterol; 1 g Carbohydrate; trace Fibre; 0 g Protein; 77 mg Sodium

Pictured on page 83 and on page 177.

Roma Lime Salsa

A food processor makes quick work of chopping the veggies. Give this away in a Mexican gift basket, page 180. Or put it together with some Chili-Jack Biscotti, page 112, for a thoughtful hostess gift. Feliz Navidad!

Chopped Roma (plum) tomatoes	7 cups	1.75 L
Chopped onion	1 cup	250 mL
Bay leaf	1	1
Ground cumin	2 tsp.	10 mL
Coarse (pickling) salt	2 tsp.	10 mL
Chili powder	1 1/2 tsp.	7 mL
Ground coriander	1 1/2 tsp.	7 mL
Dried basil	1 1/2 tsp.	7 mL
Garlic cloves, minced (or 3/4 tsp., 4 mL, powder)	3	3
Dried whole oregano	1 tsp.	5 mL
Dried thyme	1 tsp.	5 mL
Pepper	1 tsp.	5 mL
Diced green pepper	1 1/2 cups	375 mL
Lime juice	2/3 cup	150 mL
Diced celery	1/2 cup	125 mL
Jalapeño peppers, seeds and ribs removed (see Tip, page 84), diced	3	3
Granulated sugar	1 tbsp.	15 mL

Combine first 12 ingredients in large pot or Dutch oven. Heat and stir on medium-high for about 5 minutes until boiling. Reduce heat to medium-low. Simmer, uncovered, for 20 to 30 minutes, stirring occasionally, until slightly thickened.

Add remaining 5 ingredients. Stir. Bring to a boil on medium-high. Reduce heat to medium-low. Heat and stir for about 10 minutes until vegetables start to soften. Remove from heat. Discard bay leaf. Fill 6 hot sterile 1/2 pint (250 mL) jars to within 1/2 inch (12 mm) of top. Wipe rims. Place sterile metal lids on jars and screw on metal bands fingertip tight. Do not over-tighten. Process in boiling water bath for 20 minutes (see Note). Remove jars. Cool. Chill after opening. Makes about 6 cups (1.5 L).

1 tbsp. (15 mL): 6 Calories; 0.1 g Total Fat (0 g Mono, 0 g Poly, 0 g Sat); 0 mg Cholesterol; 1 g Carbohydrate; trace Fibre; 0 g Protein; 50 mg Sodium

Pictured on page 83 and on page 181.

Note: Processing time is for elevations 1001 to 3000 feet (306 to 915 m) above sea level. Make adjustment for elevation in your area if necessary.

Top Left: Chili-Jack Biscotti, page 112
Top Right: Roma Lime Salsa, above
Bottom Right: Wheat And Walnut Crackers, page 110
Bottom Left: Tapenade Salsa, this page

"Rhuby" Ginger Marmalade

Ginger and rhubarb make an interesting, flavourful pair. Serve on English muffins or biscuits for a sweet, satisfying snack or give with the Sesame Health Loaf Mix, page 51.

Frozen rhubarb, chopped smaller	4 cups	1 L
Granulated sugar	3 cups	750 mL
Grated zest and juice of 2 medium oranges		
Finely grated, peeled gingerroot	1 tbsp.	15 mL

Combine all 4 ingredients in large pot or Dutch oven. Heat on medium-low for 20 to 25 minutes, stirring occasionally, until sugar is dissolved. Bring to a rolling boil on medium. Boil for 20 to 25 minutes, stirring often, until mixture gels. To test, remove rhubarb mixture from heat. Transfer small amount to ice-cold plate. Place in freezer for 2 minutes. If mixture gels, it is ready for canning. If not, return rhubarb mixture to heat and simmer for 10 minutes. Retest for gelling. Remove from heat. Fill 2 hot sterile 1/2 pint (250 mL) jars to within 1/4 inch (6 mm) of top. Wipe rims. Place sterile metal lids on jars and screw on metal bands fingertip tight. Do not over-tighten. Process in boiling water bath for 15 minutes (see Note). Remove jars. Cool. Chill after opening. Makes about 2 cups (500 mL).

1 tbsp. (15 mL): 80 Calories; 0 g Total Fat (0 g Mono, 0 g Poly, 0 g Sat); 0 mg Cholesterol; 21 g Carbohydrate; trace Fibre; 0 g Protein; 1 mg Sodium

Pictured on page 51.

Note: Processing time is for elevations 1001 to 3000 feet (306 to 915 m) above sea level. Make adjustment for elevation in your area if necessary.

Two Berry Jam

Two berries are better than one! A splash of raspberry liqueur rounds out the flavour. A student at college will enjoy getting this in a College Care Package, page 176.

Granulated sugar	4 cups	1 L
Finely chopped frozen raspberries	2 cups	500 mL
Finely chopped frozen strawberries	2 cups	500 mL
Lemon juice	2 tbsp.	30 mL
Pouch of liquid pectin	3 oz.	85 mL
Raspberry-flavoured liqueur (such as Chambord), optional	1/4 cup	60 mL

Combine first 4 ingredients in large pot or Dutch oven. Let stand for 10 minutes. Heat and stir on high for 8 to 10 minutes until boiling and sugar is dissolved. Remove from heat.

Add pectin and liqueur. Stir well. Fill 5 hot sterile 1/2 pint (250 mL) jars to within 1/4 inch (6 mm) of top. Wipe rims. Place sterile metal lids on jars and screw on metal bands fingertip tight. Do not over-tighten. Process in boiling water bath for 15 minutes (see Note). Remove jars. Cool. Chill after opening. Makes about 5 cups (1.25 L).

1 tbsp. (15 mL): 45 Calories; 0 g Total Fat (0 g Mono, 0 g Poly, 0 g Sat); 0 mg Cholesterol; 12 g Carbohydrate; trace Fibre; 0 g Protein; 1 mg Sodium

Pictured on page 85 and on page 176.

Note: Processing time is for elevations 1001 to 3000 feet (306 to 915 m) above sea level. Make adjustment for elevation in your area if necessary.

Tip: Hot peppers contain capsaicin in the seeds and ribs. To reduce heat, remove the seeds and ribs. Wear rubber gloves when handling hot peppers and avoid touching your eyes. Wash your hands well afterwards.

Fiesta Relish

In a pickle about a gift to give? This tangy corn relish speckled with dill brightens up a Mexican gift basket, page 180. Or you can tuck it into a basket with Tijuana Triangles, Pita Scoops and Spiced Crackers—all recipes found on page 106.

White vinegar	3/4 cup	175 mL
Apple cider vinegar	1/2 cup	125 mL
Granulated sugar	1/3 cup	75 mL
Coarse (pickling) salt	1/2 tsp.	2 mL
Ground cumin	1/2 tsp.	2 mL
Yellow mustard seed	1/2 tsp.	2 mL
Pepper	1/2 tsp.	2 mL
Frozen kernel corn	4 cups	1 L
Finely chopped red onion	1/2 cup	125 mL
Finely chopped green pepper	1/2 cup	125 mL
Finely chopped red pepper	1/2 cup	125 mL
Jalapeño pepper (with seeds), finely diced (see Tip, page 84)	1	1
Garlic cloves, minced (or 1/2 tsp., 2 mL, powder)	2	2
Water	3 tbsp.	50 mL
All-purpose flour	2 tbsp.	30 mL
Chopped fresh dill	1 tbsp.	15 mL

Combine first 7 ingredients in large pot or Dutch oven. Heat and stir on high until boiling.

Add next 6 ingredients. Stir well. Bring to a boil.

Stir water into flour in small cup until smooth. Add to corn mixture. Heat and stir on medium for about 5 minutes until boiling and thickened. Remove from heat.

Add dill. Stir well. Fill 4 hot sterile 1/2 pint (250 mL) jars to within 1/2 inch (12 mm) of top. Wipe rims. Place sterile metal lids on jars and screw on metal bands fingertip tight. Do not over-tighten. Process in boiling water bath for 15 minutes (see Note). Remove jars. Cool. Chill after opening. Makes about 4 cups (1 L).

1 tbsp. (15 mL): 16 Calories; 0.1 g Total Fat (0 g Mono, 0 g Poly, 0 g Sat); 0 mg Cholesterol; 4 g Carbohydrate; trace Fibre; 0 g Protein; 18 mg Sodium

Pictured on page 107, on page 181 and on back cover.

Note: Processing time is for elevations 1001 to 3000 feet (306 to 915 m) above sea level. Make adjustment for elevation in your area if necessary.

Two Berry Jam, page 84

Beet Relish

*A sweet and pungent pairing—tart apples
and sugary beets—makes a pretty purple relish
and a great hostess gift.*

Fresh beets	2 lbs.	900 g
Tart medium cooking apples (such as Granny Smith), peeled, cores removed, diced (about 4 cups, 1 L)	4	4
Chopped onion	2 cups	500 mL
Granulated sugar	2 cups	500 mL
White vinegar	2 cups	500 mL
Ground ginger	1 tbsp.	15 mL
Dry mustard	1 tbsp.	15 mL
Salt	2 tsp.	10 mL
Pepper	1/2 tsp.	2 mL

Wrap beets individually with foil. Place on baking sheet. Bake in 350°F (175°C) oven for about 1 1/2 hours, depending on size of beets, until tender. Let stand until cool enough to handle. Discard foil. Peel beets. Chop. Transfer to large pot or Dutch oven.

Add remaining 8 ingredients. Heat and stir on medium for about 15 minutes until boiling and sugar is dissolved. Boil gently, uncovered, for about 20 minutes, stirring occasionally, until starting to thicken. Reduce heat to medium-low. Simmer, uncovered, for about 10 minutes, stirring occasionally, until liquid is almost evaporated. Remove from heat. Fill 5 hot sterile 1/2 pint (250 mL) jars to within 1/2 inch (12 mm) of top. Wipe rims. Place sterile metal lids on jars and screw on metal bands fingertip tight. Do not over-tighten. Process in boiling water bath for 15 minutes (see Note). Remove jars. Cool. Store for up to 2 months. Chill after opening. Makes about 5 cups (1.25 L).

1 tbsp. (15 mL): 30 Calories; 0.1 g Total Fat (0 g Mono, 0 g Poly, 0 g Sat); 0 mg Cholesterol; 8 g Carbohydrate; trace Fibre; 0 g Protein; 65 mg Sodium

Pictured on page 87.

Note: Processing time is for elevations 1001 to 3000 feet (306 to 915 m) above sea level. Make adjustment for elevation in your area if necessary.

Zucchini Relish

*Tastes great on burgers, hot dogs and sandwiches.
Nestle a jar of this zippy relish in a Barbecue gift basket,
page 180. Add a comical apron for a great gift for Dad!*

Finely chopped zucchini (with peel)	4 cups	1 L
Finely chopped onion	1 cup	250 mL
Finely chopped green pepper	1/2 cup	125 mL
Coarse (pickling) salt	2 tbsp.	30 mL
Cold water		
Granulated sugar	1 1/2 cups	375 mL
Apple cider vinegar	3/4 cup	175 mL
White vinegar	1/2 cup	125 mL
Celery seed	2 tsp.	10 mL
Yellow mustard seed	1 tsp.	5 mL
Dried crushed chilies	1/2 tsp.	2 mL
Ground allspice	1/2 tsp.	2 mL
Dry mustard	1/2 tsp.	2 mL
Jar of roasted red peppers, drained, blotted dry, finely chopped	13 oz.	370 mL

Combine zucchini, onion and green pepper in large bowl. Sprinkle with salt. Add cold water until 2 inches (5 cm) above vegetables. Let stand for 1 hour. Drain. Press to remove excess water. Set aside.

Measure next 8 ingredients into large pot or Dutch oven. Stir well. Bring to a boil on high.

Add zucchini mixture and red pepper. Stir. Bring to a boil. Reduce heat to medium-low. Simmer, uncovered, for about 1 hour, stirring occasionally, until liquid is almost evaporated. Remove from heat. Fill 4 hot sterile 1/2 pint (250 mL) jars to within 1/2 inch (12 mm) of top. Wipe rims. Place sterile metal lids on jars and screw on metal bands fingertip tight. Do not over-tighten. Process in boiling water bath for 15 minutes (see Note). Remove jars. Cool. Chill after opening. Makes about 4 cups (1 L).

1 tbsp. (15 mL): 22 Calories; 0 g Total Fat (0 g Mono, 0 g Poly, 0 g Sat); 0 mg Cholesterol; 6 g Carbohydrate; trace Fibre; 0 g Protein; 107 mg Sodium

Pictured on page 87.

Note: Processing time is for elevations 1001 to 3000 feet (306 to 915 m) above sea level. Make adjustment for elevation in your area if necessary.

Left: Beet Relish, this page, and Bird Nest Jar Topper, page 88
Right: Zucchini Relish, above, and Pompom Jar Topper, page 88

✳ Pompom Jar Topper ✳

Put a festive touch on your jars with this easy-to-make decorative topper. Get the kids to help glue on the pompoms for a fun family project.

MATERIALS
Jar with lid
Peel-and-stick felt piece (9 x 12 inches, 22 x 30 cm)
White fun fur
Package of glitter multi-coloured pompoms (1/2 inch, 12 mm, diameter)

TOOLS
pencil, scissors, cloth tape measure, stapler, white craft glue

Trace the lid onto the backing of the felt and cut out the circle. Peel off the backing and secure the felt to the top of the jar lid.

Measure the height and circumference of the lid for the fur, adding 1/2 inch (12 mm) to the circumference measurement for stapling. Cut the fur to fit. Wrap the fur around the lid, slightly overlapping the ends. Remove the fur from the lid, holding ends tightly together. Staple the overlapped fur. Slide the fur back onto the lid.

Glue the pompoms to the felt on top of the lid, spiralling from the outside and working toward the centre.

Pictured on page 87.

✳ Bird Nest Jar Topper ✳

This topper adds an attractive, seasonal touch to your gift in a jar. Be sure to use a craft bird in a colour that complements the jar's contents.

MATERIALS
Jar with lid
Peel-and-stick felt piece (9 x 12 inches, 22 x 30 cm)
Gold twig wreath (3 1/2 inch, 9 cm, diameter)
Natural raffia
Pinecone with snow craft pick
Berry spray craft pick
Medium-sized craft bird

TOOLS
pencil, scissors, glue gun, wire cutters

Trace the lid onto the backing of the felt and cut out the circle. Peel off the backing and secure the felt to the top of the jar lid.

Centre the wreath on the lid. Lightly trace the inside of the wreath onto the felt. Put glue along the outside of the traced circle. Secure the wreath to the felt.

Put 3 dabs of glue inside the nest. Bundle up some raffia and place it on top of the glue inside the nest. Cut a few pieces of pine off the craft pick. Cut a few berries off the spray craft pick. Glue the pine, berries and the bird to the inside of the nest.

Pictured on page 87.

Left and Bottom Centre: A Crock Of Cheese, below

Right and Bottom Centre: Caraway Wheat Crackers, page 105

A Crock Of Cheese

Smooth and creamy, with a nip of mustard and garlic. A lovely gift, with the chopped pecans packaged separately in a cellophane bag and put in a decorative box with the Crock of Cheese, Caraway Wheat Crackers, page 105, cocktail napkins and a spreader. Bon Appetit!

Blocks of cream cheese (8 oz., 250 g, each), softened	2	2
Grated sharp Cheddar cheese	2 cups	500 mL
Dijon-flavoured mayonnaise (see Note)	2 tbsp.	30 mL
Parsley flakes	1 tbsp.	15 mL
Garlic clove, minced (or 1/4 tsp., 1 mL, powder), optional	1	1
Coarse ground pepper	1/2 tsp.	2 mL
Coarsely chopped pecans, toasted (see Tip, page 22)	2 tbsp.	30 mL

Process first 6 ingredients in food processor until smooth. Spoon into decorative airtight container. Smooth top.

Store in refrigerator for up to 10 days or freeze for up to 3 months. Serve at room temperature. Just before serving, sprinkle with pecans. Makes about 2 2/3 cups (650 mL).

1 tbsp. (15 mL): 66 Calories; 6.2 g Total Fat (1.9 g Mono, 0.4 g Poly, 3.7 g Sat); 18 mg Cholesterol; 0 g Carbohydrate; trace Fibre; 2 g Protein; 73 mg Sodium

Pictured above.

Note: To make your own Dijon-flavoured mayonnaise, combine 4 tsp. (20 mL) mayonnaise and 2 tsp. (10 mL) Dijon mustard in small cup.

Spiced German Mustard

A medium-hot mustard that's perfect for bratwurst.
Add heat by simmering longer to further reduce the volume
and condense the flavour. Makes a great hostess gift.

Cold water	1/2 cup	125 mL
Yellow mustard seed	1/3 cup	75 mL
Dry mustard	1/4 cup	60 mL
Apple cider vinegar	1 cup	250 mL
Finely chopped onion	1/2 cup	125 mL
Brown sugar, packed	2 tbsp.	30 mL
Garlic cloves, minced	2	2
(or 1/2 tsp., 2 mL, powder)		
Salt	1 tsp.	5 mL
Ground cinnamon	1/2 tsp.	2 mL
Ground allspice	1/4 tsp.	1 mL
Dill weed	1/4 tsp.	1 mL
Dried tarragon leaves	1/4 tsp.	1 mL
Turmeric	1/8 tsp.	0.5 mL
Liquid honey	1 tbsp.	15 mL

Combine cold water, mustard seed and dry mustard in medium bowl. Cover. Let stand for about 3 hours until mixture thickens to a paste.

Combine next 10 ingredients in medium saucepan. Bring to a boil on medium-high. Reduce heat to medium. Simmer, uncovered, for 10 to 15 minutes, stirring often, until reduced by half. Add to mustard mixture. Stir. Transfer to blender or food processor. Pulse with on/off motion until mustard is slightly thickened but grains are still visible. Pour into small heavy saucepan or top of double boiler. Heat on medium-low or over simmering water for 10 to 15 minutes, stirring occasionally, until thickened. Remove from heat.

Add honey. Stir well. Cool. Transfer to small bowl. Cover. Chill for 3 days. Spoon into sterile jar with tight-fitting lid. Store in refrigerator for up to 2 years. Makes about 1 cup (250 mL).

2 tsp. (10 mL): 31 Calories; 1.3 g Total Fat (0.9 g Mono, 0.2 g Poly, 0.1 g Sat);
0 mg Cholesterol; 4 g Carbohydrate; trace Fibre; 1 g Protein; 96 mg Sodium

Pictured on this page.

Left: Apple Honey Vinaigrette, page 91
Right: Spiced German Mustard, above

Raspberry Thyme Vinegar

*A vibrant red vinegar with a pleasant, tangy acidity.
A great choice drizzled on crisp greens or mixed with
olive oil for dipping. Gift in a decorative bottle and give
with the Parmesan Herb Focaccia Mix, page 48.*

White wine vinegar	4 cups	1 L
Fresh (or frozen, thawed) raspberries	1 cup	250 mL
Granulated sugar	1/4 cup	60 mL
Sprigs of fresh thyme (or 1 tsp., 5 mL, dried)	4	4

Combine all 4 ingredients in 6 cup (1.5 L) jar with
tight-fitting lid. Let stand at room temperature for 2 weeks.
Strain through sieve into large bowl. Do not press. Gently lift
raspberry mixture with spoon, allowing liquid to flow through
sieve. Discard solids. Strain liquid again through double layer
of cheesecloth into 4 cup (1 L) liquid measure. Pour into
sterile jars or cruets with tight-fitting lids. Store in refrigerator
for up to 1 month. Makes about 4 1/3 cups (1.1 L).

1 tbsp. (15 mL): 6 Calories; 0 g Total Fat (0 g Mono, 0 g Poly, 0 g Sat);
  0 mg Cholesterol; 2 g Carbohydrate; trace Fibre; 0 g Protein; 0 mg Sodium

Pictured on page 49.

Apple Honey Vinaigrette

*A pretty pale yellow dressing flecked with pepper.
Makes a delicious Christmas gift for a special hostess.
Don't forget add a label saying, "Shake well before using."*

Cooking oil	2 cups	500 mL
Apple cider vinegar	2/3 cup	150 mL
Apple juice	1/3 cup	75 mL
Liquid honey	3 tbsp.	50 mL
Dijon mustard	2 tbsp.	30 mL
Salt	1/4 tsp.	1 mL
Pepper	1/4 tsp.	1 mL

Process all 7 ingredients in blender until well combined.
Pour into sterile jars or decorative bottles with tight-fitting
lids. Store in refrigerator for up to 1 month. Shake well before
using. Makes about 3 1/3 cups (825 mL).

1 tbsp. (15 mL): 79 Calories; 8.3 g Total Fat (4.9 g Mono, 2.5 g Poly, 0.6 g Sat);
  0 mg Cholesterol; 1 g Carbohydrate; 0 g Fibre; 0 g Protein; 18 mg Sodium

Pictured on page 90.

Cilantro Sunflower Pesto

*Garlic, chili pepper and a splash of lime add zip to cilantro.
A great little pesto to add to pasta, sauces and dips. Spoon
it into a pretty jar and top the lid with a silk sunflower.*

Chopped fresh cilantro, lightly packed	4 cups	1 L
Unsalted roasted sunflower seeds	1/2 cup	125 mL
Fresh chili pepper (with seeds), see Note	1	1
Garlic cloves	3	3
Grated lime zest	2 tsp.	10 mL
Olive (or cooking) oil	1/4 cup	60 mL

Process first 5 ingredients in food processor until finely
chopped.

With motor running, add olive oil in thin stream through feed
chute until mixture is thick and grainy. Spoon into sterile jar
with tight-fitting lid. Store for up to 2 weeks in refrigerator
(see Note). Makes about 1 cup (250 mL).

1 tbsp. (15 mL): 66 Calories; 5.9 g Total Fat (3 g Mono, 1.8 g Poly, 0.7 g Sat);
  0 mg Cholesterol; 2 g Carbohydrate; 1 g Fibre; 2 g Protein; 11 mg Sodium

Pictured below and on back cover.

Note: Use your favourite type of chili pepper based on the
amount of heat you desire. Generally, the smaller the pepper,
the hotter its flavour. If preferred, omit fresh chili pepper, and
use up to 1/2 tsp. (2 mL) dried crushed chilies.

Note: After chilling, surface of pesto will darken. This does
not affect the taste. If desired, skim off and discard.

Berry Christmas Sauce

This fruity sauce makes a great gift and can be used over ice cream, pancakes or French toast.

Frozen strawberries	1 cup	250 mL
Frozen raspberries	1 cup	250 mL
Granulated sugar	1 cup	250 mL
Apple juice	3/4 cup	175 mL
Frozen blueberries	1/2 cup	125 mL
Frozen blackberries	1/2 cup	125 mL
Lemon juice	1 tbsp.	15 mL
Apple juice	1/4 cup	60 mL
Cornstarch	2 tbsp.	30 mL

Combine first 7 ingredients in medium saucepan. Heat and stir on medium until boiling. Reduce heat to medium-low. Simmer, uncovered, for about 10 minutes, stirring occasionally, until fruit is softened.

Stir second amount of apple juice into cornstarch in small cup until smooth. Add to berry mixture, stirring constantly. Heat and stir for 3 to 4 minutes until sauce is boiling and thickened. Pour into sterile bottles with tight-fitting lids. Store in refrigerator for up to 1 month. Makes about 2 1/2 cups (625 mL).

1 tbsp. (15 mL): 30 Calories; 0.1 g Total Fat (0 g Mono, 0 g Poly, 0 g Sat); 0 mg Cholesterol; 8 g Carbohydrate; trace Fibre; 0 g Protein; 0 mg Sodium

Pictured on page 93.

Butterscotch Sauce

An ideal gift for ice cream lovers! Label: Stir well before using.

Brown sugar, packed	1 cup	250 mL
Golden corn syrup	2/3 cup	150 mL
Hard margarine (or butter)	1/4 cup	60 mL
Can of evaporated milk	5 1/2 oz.	160 mL
Vanilla	1 tsp.	5 mL

Heat and stir brown sugar, corn syrup and margarine in medium saucepan on medium for about 7 minutes until margarine is melted and mixture is boiling. Boil gently, uncovered, for 1 minute, without stirring. Remove from heat. Let stand for 5 minutes.

Add evaporated milk and vanilla. Stir well. Pour into sterile bottles with tight-fitting lids. Store in refrigerator for up to 1 month. Stir well before using. Makes about 2 cups (500 mL).

1 tbsp. (15 mL): 66 Calories; 1.9 g Total Fat (1.1 g Mono, 0.2 g Poly, 0.5 g Sat); 2 mg Cholesterol; 13 g Carbohydrate; 0 g Fibre; 0 g Protein; 34 mg Sodium

Pictured on page 93 and on page 173.

Orange Liqueur Sauce

A sweet, shiny sauce. Serve over ice cream, crêpes or waffles. Add a bow to the bottle and it's a scrumptious gift!

Brown sugar, packed	1/3 cup	75 mL
Cornstarch	1 1/2 tbsp.	25 mL
Orange juice	1 cup	250 mL
Orange-flavoured liqueur (such as Grand Marnier)	2 tbsp.	30 mL

Combine brown sugar and cornstarch in microwave-safe 2 cup (500 mL) liquid measure. Slowly add orange juice, stirring constantly until smooth. Microwave, uncovered, on high (100%) for 2 minutes. Stir. Microwave on high (100%) for 1 to 1 1/2 minutes until boiling and thickened. Let stand for 10 minutes.

Add liqueur. Stir well. Pour into sterile bottle with tight-fitting lid. Store in refrigerator for up to 2 weeks. Makes about 1 1/4 cups (300 mL).

1 tbsp. (15 mL): 25 Calories; 0 g Total Fat (0 g Mono, 0 g Poly, 0 g Sat); 0 mg Cholesterol; 5 g Carbohydrate; trace Fibre; 0 g Protein; 2 mg Sodium

Pictured on page 37 and on page 172.

Chocolate Liqueur Sauce

Something special to include in a Chocolate Lover's gift basket, page 172. Add to hot milk for a warm winter beverage or use as a decadent dessert topping.

Whipping cream	2 cups	500 mL
Dark chocolate bars (3 1/2 oz., 100 g, each), coarsely chopped	4	4
Hard margarine (or butter)	1/2 cup	125 mL
Coffee-flavoured liqueur (such as Kahlúa)	1/3 cup	75 mL
Dark corn syrup	3 tbsp.	50 mL

Heat whipping cream in heavy medium saucepan on medium until hot and bubbles form around edge. Remove from heat.

Add remaining 4 ingredients. Stir until smooth. Cool. Pour into sterile jars with tight-fitting lids. Store in refrigerator for up to 1 month. Makes about 4 cups (1 L).

1 tbsp. (15 mL): 72 Calories; 5.7 g Total Fat (2.3 g Mono, 0.3 g Poly, 2.9 g Sat); 9 mg Cholesterol; 5 g Carbohydrate; trace Fibre; 0 g Protein; 22 mg Sodium

Pictured on page 93 and on page 175.

Top Left: Chocolate Liqueur Sauce, above
Top Right: Butterscotch Sauce, this page
Centre: Berry Christmas Sauce, this page

Tropical Cream Liqueur

Bottle this thick, creamy rum and pineapple-flavoured liqueur in an attractive container. Place in a Sun-Seeker's gift basket, page 182, with freshly baked Christmas goodies. Or wrap with cellophane and tie with a bow—a great gift on its own.

Can of crushed pineapple (with juice)	14 oz.	398 mL
Ripe medium bananas	2	2
Lime juice	1 tsp.	5 mL
Can of coconut cream	14 oz.	398 mL
Can of sweetened condensed milk	11 oz.	300 mL
Cans of evaporated milk (13 1/2 oz., 385 mL, each)	2	2
Bottle of white (light) rum	13 1/4 oz.	375 mL
Bottle of vodka	13 1/4 oz.	375 mL

Process pineapple with juice, bananas and lime juice in blender or food processor until smooth.

Add coconut cream and condensed milk. Process for about 1 minute until well combined. Transfer to large bowl.

Add evaporated milk, rum and vodka. Stir well. Chill overnight. Stir. Pour into sterile jars or decorative bottles with tight-fitting lids. Store in refrigerator for up to 1 month. Makes about 8 1/2 cups (2.1 L).

1 oz. (30 mL): 82 Calories; 3.4 g Total Fat (0.5 g Mono, 0.1 g Poly, 2.6 g Sat); 5 mg Cholesterol; 6 g Carbohydrate; trace Fibre; 1 g Protein; 20 mg Sodium

Pictured on page 95 and on page 183.

> **Directions for Tropical Dream:**
>
> Pour 1 to 2 oz. (30 to 60 mL) Tropical Cream Liqueur over ice in medium glass. Add orange juice or lemon lime soft drink until full.

Cranberry Lemon Sipper

A beautifully clear, deep red apéritif to sip while basting the Christmas turkey. Get a head start on this recipe, so this can macerate or blend. Add directions for the spritzer on the gift, and toast the New Year with friends.

Fresh (or frozen, thawed) cranberries	4 cups	1 L
Granulated sugar	2 cups	500 mL
Water	1 cup	250 mL
Sweet white wine (such as Gewürztraminer)	2 cups	500 mL
Bottle of vodka	13 1/4 oz.	375 mL
Grated zest and juice of 1 medium lemon		

Combine cranberries, sugar and water in large saucepan. Heat and stir on high until boiling. Reduce heat to medium. Boil gently, uncovered, for 5 to 10 minutes, stirring occasionally, until cranberries are softened. Remove from heat.

Add remaining 3 ingredients. Stir well. Cool. Pour into 10 cup (2.5 L) jar with tight-fitting lid. Let stand at room temperature for 3 weeks, shaking gently once every 2 days. Strain through sieve into large bowl. Do not press. Gently lift cranberry mixture with spoon, allowing liquid to flow through sieve. Discard solids. Strain liquid again through double layer of cheesecloth into 8 cup (2 L) liquid measure. Pour into sterile jars or decorative bottles with tight-fitting lids. Store at room temperature for up to 1 month to mature. Chill after opening. Makes about 4 1/3 cups (1.1 L).

1 oz. (30 mL): 84 Calories; 0 g Total Fat (0 g Mono, 0 g Poly, 0 g Sat); 0 mg Cholesterol; 14 g Carbohydrate; trace Fibre; 0 g Protein; 1 mg Sodium

Pictured on page 78 and on page 95.

> **Directions for Cranberry Lemon Sipper:**
>
> Pour over crushed ice in small glass.
>
>
>
> **Directions for Cranberry Lemon Spritzer:**
>
> Pour Cranberry Lemon Sipper over ice in large glass until 1/2 to 2/3 full. Fill with ginger ale, club soda or sparkling bottled water (such as Perrier).

Top Left: Cranberry Lemon Sipper, above
Right: Tropical Cream Liqueur, this page
Bottom Left: Cranberry Lemon Spritzer, above

Kits for Kids

Even as the festive season grows busier, don't forget to set aside some time with excited little ones to create lasting memories together. These ingenious kits will keep young hands busy and happy when school lets out for the holidays. Parents and children can work together to create a beautiful Christmas centrepiece to enjoy during the holidays.

Here's another great idea—think about offering one or more of these kits as a gift to grandparents, aunts and uncles, along with the opportunity to spend some time with young family members. You may be starting a wonderful holiday tradition that will endure for years to come.

Candy Christmas Tree Kit

A gift to make with the kids!
They'll love spending time with their
parents or grandparents creating this
"masterpiece" of Christmas art.

ROYAL ICING

Icing (confectioner's) sugar	2 2/3 cups	650 mL
Water	1/4 cup	60 mL
Meringue powder (see Note)	2 tbsp.	30 mL
Leaf-shaped spearmint gumdrops, halved horizontally	1 cup	250 mL

Red licorice string

Yellow gumdrop

Large silver dragées
Assorted coloured candies

MATERIALS
Styrofoam cone (3 x 6 inches, 7.5 x 15 cm)
Foiled cake board (5 x 5 inches, 12.5 x 12.5 cm)
2 small resealable freezer bags
Rolling pin
Miniature star cookie cutter

Royal Icing: Beat icing sugar, water and meringue powder in large bowl for about 1 minute until stiff peaks form.

Spread small amount of icing on bottom of cone. Press onto centre of cake board to secure. Let stand until set. Spoon remaining icing into 2 resealable freezer bags with tiny piece snipped off corner, or into 2 paper cones (page 27). Set 1 bag aside until needed.

Pipe generous amount of icing on cut-side of 1 gumdrop leaf half. Press leaf, narrow-end down, onto cone, about 1/4 inch (6 mm) from top edge. Allow icing to squeeze out onto cone. Repeat, placing leaves in single row, narrow-ends down, around entire top edge of cone. Repeat with remaining leaf halves, working down from top, one row at a time until cone is covered. Let stand until set.

Wrap licorice string around wooden spoon handle. Hold in place for about 30 seconds to shape licorice. Unwind. Pipe icing on 1 end of licorice string. Press on top of tree to secure. Hold in place for 1 to 2 minutes until set. Wrap licorice around tree toward base to form garland. Pipe icing on opposite end of licorice string. Press onto tree to secure. Hold in place for 1 to 2 minutes until set. Let stand overnight until set.

Flatten yellow gumdrop with rolling pin or flat-bottomed glass. Cut out star shape with miniature cookie cutter or cut into star shape with kitchen scissors or knife. Secure star with icing to top of tree. Hold in place for 1 to 2 minutes until set.

Pipe remaining icing on dragées and coloured candies 1 at a time, pressing onto or between leaves, decorating as desired. Let stand until set. Makes 1 candy tree.

Pictured below.

Note: Meringue powder can be purchased at specialty kitchen stores or wherever cake decorating supplies are sold.

Graham Cracker House Kit

A project kids will love. You may want to make this a bit early in the season so kids can enjoy their prized centrepiece throughout the holiday. Let them gobble it up as a Boxing Day treat. A bit of parental help will make it fun for all!

ROYAL ICING

Icing (confectioner's) sugar	2 2/3 cups	650 mL
Water	1/4 cup	60 mL
Meringue powder (see Note)	2 tbsp.	30 mL
Small resealable freezer bags	2	2
Whole graham cracker squares	49	49

DECORATING SUGGESTIONS

Candy canes
Sugar-coated jujubes and jelly candies
Red licorice strings
Square chocolate mints
Mini cream-filled cookies
Assorted ice wafer cookies
Small bow tie or stick pretzels
Rice or wheat squares cereal
Small fruit-flavoured candies (such as Skittles)
Assorted hard candies (such as Lifesavers or Scotch mints)
Large marshmallows
Miniature multi-coloured marshmallows
Icing (confectioner's) sugar, for dusting

MATERIALS

Foiled cake board (12 × 15 inches, 30 × 38 cm), or board covered with decorative paper

Royal Icing: Beat icing sugar, water and meringue powder in large bowl for about 1 minute until stiff peaks form. Spoon into 2 resealable freezer bags with tiny piece snipped off corner, or into 2 paper cones (page 27). Set 1 bag aside until needed.

HOUSE PIECES

Base And Side Walls: Lay 6 crackers right-side up on work surface, with edges touching, to make a rectangle 3 crackers long and 2 crackers wide. Pipe icing between crackers. Gently press edges together. Let stand until set (Royal Icing will harden quickly). Repeat twice, for a total of 1 base and 2 side walls.

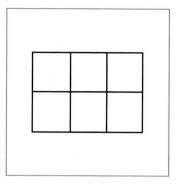

End Walls: Lay 4 crackers right-side up on work surface, with edges touching, to make a square. Pipe icing between crackers. Gently press edges together. Let stand until set. Repeat, for a total of 2 end walls.

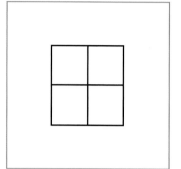

Cut 1 cracker in half diagonally. Lay halves right-side up on work surface, with short edges touching, to make 1 large triangle. Pipe icing between halves. Gently press edges together. Let stand until set. Repeat, for a total of 2 gables.

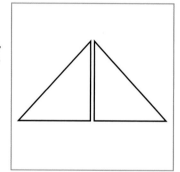

Lay long side of 1 gable along 1 edge of end wall, right-side up on work surface, with edges touching. Pipe icing between aligned edges and gently press together to attach end wall to gable. Repeat, for a total of 2 end walls.

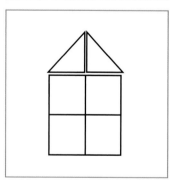

Roof: Lay 4 crackers right-side up on work surface, with edges touching, to make a long rectangle. Pipe icing between crackers. Gently press edges together. Let stand until set. Repeat 3 times, for a total of 4 roof rectangles.

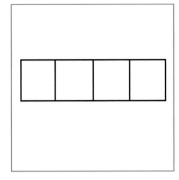

Doors And Windows: Cut crackers into small rectangles or squares, as desired. Pipe icing onto right-side of crackers to make door knobs or window panes. Let stand until set.

ASSEMBLY

Place base of house on work surface, right-side down. Pipe icing on base along all 4 sides near edge. Pipe dabs of icing along centre of base. Position base, icing-side down, on top of cake board. Press gently to secure. Let stand until set.

Pipe icing along outside edges of base on 1 long side and 1 short side. Place 1 side wall, right-side facing out, against long edge with icing. Press gently. Place 1 end wall, right-side facing out, against short edge with icing. Press gently. Hold both walls in place for 1 to 2 minutes until secure. Repeat with icing and remaining walls. Pipe icing along edges where walls meet. Gently press together to secure. Let stand until set.

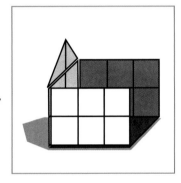

Pipe 2 lines of icing down length of 1 right-side up roof rectangle, about 1/4 inch (6 mm) apart. Place second rectangle right-side up on top of icing, overlapping 1/2 inch (12 mm). Set aside. Repeat with remaining roof rectangles, for a total of 2 roof pieces.

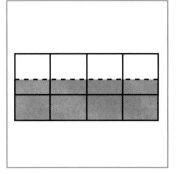

Pipe icing along 4 sloped edges of gables on end walls and along top edge of 2 side walls. Place roof pieces, right-sides facing out, on each sloped edge to form pitched roof, making sure pieces join at the peak. Hold in place for 1 to 2 minutes until secure. Carefully pipe icing at peak where roof pieces meet. Gently press together to secure. Let stand until set.

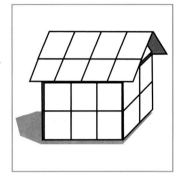

Working with door and window pieces 1 at a time, pipe some icing on wrong-side of each piece. Press onto house where desired. Hold each piece in place for 1 to 2 minutes until secure. Let stand until set.

Decorate house as desired, piping icing onto candies and gently pressing onto house. To create shingles, attach sugar-coated jelly candies, square chocolate mints or cereal squares to roof in overlapping rows using icing. Decorate cake board as desired to make a yard around house (see picture for more ideas). Let stand overnight until completely set.

Pictured on pages 100/101.

Note: Meringue powder can be purchased at specialty kitchen stores or where cake decorating supplies are sold.

Sugar Cube Igloo Kit

The kids in your life will love creating this frosty-looking winter craft! Supply some extra candy for them to nibble on while making this.

ROYAL ICING

Icing (confectioner's) sugar	2 2/3 cups	650 mL
Water	1/4 cup	60 mL
Meringue powder (see Note)	2 tbsp.	30 mL
Box of sugar cubes	1	1

PENGUINS

Small white gumdrops	4	4
Large white gumdrops	4	4
Orange jelly beans	5	5
Black licorice nibs	4	4
Red licorice strings, halved	2	2

Miniature marshmallows,
   for decoration

MATERIALS
Cardboard square (8 inches, 20 cm)
2 small resealable freezer bags
Box of sugar cubes

Draw 4 1/2 inch (11 cm) circle in centre of cardboard. Cover cardboard with plastic wrap.

Royal Icing: Beat icing sugar, water and meringue powder in large bowl for about 1 minute until stiff peaks form. Spoon into 2 resealable freezer bags with tiny piece snipped off corner, or into 2 paper cones (page 27). Set 1 bag aside until needed.

Pipe icing on plastic wrap along inside edge of circle. Press sugar cubes on top of icing about 1/8 inch (3 mm) apart. Leave space for door 2 cubes wide. Using icing, secure 2 cubes to plastic wrap outside circle on one side of the door. Repeat with 2 more cubes on the other side. Pipe icing into spaces between cubes.

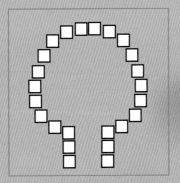

Pipe icing on top of first layer of cubes. Stagger second row of cubes slightly inward on top of first row. Repeat, staggering cubes slightly inward for a third row. Fill all spaces between cubes with icing. Repeat, forming a fourth row, closing in top of door. Add 2 more rows of cubes to enclose top of igloo (see picture). Fill in all spaces with icing. Let stand until set.

Penguins: Secure small gumdrop with icing to top of large gumdrop to form head. Cut jelly beans in half lengthwise. Secure 2 jelly bean halves, cut-sides down, with icing to bottom of large gumdrop to make feet. Let stand until set.

Cut 2 jelly bean halves crosswise, for a total of 4 pieces. Secure 1 piece with icing to small gumdrop to form beak. Set remaining pieces aside for making more penguins. Cut licorice nib lengthwise into 5 pieces. Use pieces to make 2 wings, a tail and eyes. Attach with icing (see picture below). Tie 1 licorice string half around penguin's neck to make a scarf. Repeat 3 times, for a total of 4 penguins.

Pictured on page 103.

Note: Meringue powder can be purchased at specialty kitchen stores or wherever cake decorating supplies are sold.

Savoury Snacks

One of the warmest traditions surrounding the holiday season is the prospect of reuniting with friends, family and neighbours for a bit of good cheer. These recipes can be wonderful gifts for just such an occasion. Give someone special the zesty taste of seasoned crackers, spiced nuts, cheese puffs or chips for a perfect, casual snack.

Because these recipes can be made one to two months in advance, you can begin Christmas preparations as early as November. Remember to label your gifts with "best-before"

dates to guarantee maximum freshness. Crackers can be made ahead and frozen, but if you do so, they will need to be re-crisped after thawing. Heat them on a baking sheet in a 250°F (120°C) oven for about 5 minutes.

Be bold in your gift-wrapping—fill a basket with herb-infused biscotti, wrap a hearty loaf in a Christmas tea towel, or gather a selection of tempting crackers into a decorative airtight container. There is no limit to your imagination!

Seeded Flatbread Sticks

Rustic, earthy bread sticks. Give these packaged in a cellophane bag with a jar of Curried Lentil Soup Mix, page 55—a gift to warm the heart.

All-bran cereal	1/3 cup	75 mL
Boiling water	1/4 cup	60 mL
Hard margarine (or butter), softened	1/4 cup	60 mL
Granulated sugar	1 tbsp.	15 mL
Buttermilk (or reconstituted from powder)	1/4 cup	60 mL
All-purpose flour	1 cup	250 mL
Sesame seeds, toasted (see Tip, page 22)	2 tsp.	10 mL
Flaxseed	1 tsp.	5 mL
Poppy seeds	1 tsp.	5 mL
Baking powder	1/4 tsp.	1 mL
Baking soda	1/4 tsp.	1 mL
Salt	1/8 tsp.	0.5 mL

Measure cereal into small bowl. Add boiling water. Stir. Let stand for about 10 minutes until water is absorbed.

Cream margarine and sugar in medium bowl. Add cereal mixture and buttermilk. Stir well.

Combine remaining 7 ingredients in separate small bowl. Add to cereal mixture. Mix well. Divide dough into 3 equal portions. Roll out 1 portion on lightly floured surface to 6 x 9 inch (15 x 22 cm) rectangle. Cover remaining portions to prevent drying. Cut rectangle crosswise with pizza cutter into 1/2 inch (12 mm) strips. Arrange about 1 inch (2.5 cm) apart on ungreased baking sheets. Bake in 350°F (175°C) oven for 12 to 14 minutes until edges are golden. Let stand on baking sheets for 5 minutes before removing to wire racks to cool. Cool baking sheets between batches. Repeat with remaining portions of dough. Makes about 4 1/2 dozen (54) bread sticks.

1 bread stick: 21 Calories; 1 g Total Fat (0.6 g Mono, 0.2 g Poly, 0.2 g Sat); 0 mg Cholesterol; 3 g Carbohydrate; trace Fibre; 0 g Protein; 29 mg Sodium

Pictured on page 55.

Caraway Wheat Crackers

Is someone you know a little under the weather during the holidays? Lift their spirits with a pot of homemade soup, a basket of these crispy crackers wrapped in cellophane and A Crock Of Cheese, page 89.

Whole wheat flour	3/4 cup	175 mL
All-purpose flour	1/4 cup	60 mL
Brown sugar, packed	1 tbsp.	15 mL
Caraway seed	1 tsp.	5 mL
Baking soda	1/2 tsp.	2 mL
Cooking oil	1/4 cup	60 mL
Milk	1/4 cup	60 mL
Coarse (pickling) salt	1 tsp.	5 mL

Combine first 5 ingredients in medium bowl. Make a well in centre.

Add cooking oil and milk to well. Mix well. Turn out onto lightly floured surface. Knead 6 times. Cover. Let stand for 10 minutes. Roll out dough on 11 x 15 inch (28 x 38 cm) sheet of parchment paper to 10 x 14 inch (25 x 35 cm) rectangle. Let stand for 10 minutes. Cut with pizza cutter into 1 x 2 inch (2.5 x 5 cm) rectangles. Transfer parchment paper with rectangles to 11 x 17 inch (28 x 43 cm) baking sheet.

Sprinkle salt evenly over rectangles. Bake in 425°F (220°C) oven for 6 to 8 minutes until golden. Let stand on baking sheet for 5 minutes before removing to wire rack to cool. Makes about 6 dozen (72) crackers.

1 cracker: 15 Calories; 0.9 g Total Fat (0.5 g Mono, 0.3 g Poly, 0.1 g Sat); 0 mg Cholesterol; 2 g Carbohydrate; trace Fibre; 0 g Protein; 44 mg Sodium

Pictured on page 89.

CARAWAY WHEAT CROUTONS: Cut rolled out dough with pizza cutter into 1 inch (2.5 cm) squares. Bake in 425°F (220°C) oven for 5 to 6 minutes until golden. Makes about 11 1/2 dozen (138) croutons.

Tijuana Triangles

A chip with zip! These spicy snacks make a flavourful addition to a Mexican gift basket, page 180.

Cooking oil	1 tbsp.	15 mL
Corn tortillas (6 inch, 15 cm, diameter)	12	12
Chili powder	2 tsp.	10 mL
Grated lime zest	1 tsp.	5 mL
Salt	1 tsp.	5 mL

Brush cooking oil lightly on both sides of each tortilla. Cut each tortilla into 8 wedges. Arrange in single layer on ungreased baking sheets.

Combine chili powder, lime zest and salt in small cup. Sprinkle evenly over tortilla wedges. Bake in 350°F (175°C) oven for 10 to 12 minutes until golden. Cool. Makes 8 dozen (96) triangles.

1 triangle: 8 Calories; 0.2 g Total Fat (0.1 g Mono, 0.1 g Poly, 0 g Sat); 0 mg Cholesterol; 1 g Carbohydrate; trace Fibre; 0 g Protein; 30 mg Sodium

Pictured on page 107 and on page 181.

Pita Scoops

A spicy snack for scooping salsa. Give a bag of these in a Snack Attack gift basket, page 177, with a jar of Tapenade Salsa, page 82.

Pita breads (3 inch, 7.5 cm, diameter), each cut into 4 wedges	18	18
Olive (or cooking) oil	2 tbsp.	30 mL
Grated Parmesan cheese	1/2 cup	125 mL
Chili powder	2 tsp.	10 mL
Seasoned salt	1 tsp.	5 mL
Onion powder	1/2 tsp.	2 mL
Garlic powder	1/2 tsp.	2 mL
Cayenne pepper	1/2 tsp.	2 mL

Put pita wedges into extra-large bowl. Drizzle with olive oil. Toss until coated.

Combine remaining 6 ingredients in small bowl. Sprinkle 1/2 of mixture over pita wedges. Toss. Sprinkle with remaining spice mixture. Toss well. Arrange in single layer on greased baking sheets. Bake in 350°F (175°C) oven for 10 to 15 minutes until golden. Cool. Makes 6 dozen (72) pita scoops.

1 pita scoop: 17 Calories; 0.7 g Total Fat (0.4 g Mono, 0.1 g Poly, 0.2 g Sat); 1 mg Cholesterol; 2 g Carbohydrate; trace Fibre; 1 g Protein; 51 mg Sodium

Pictured on page 107 and on page 177.

Spiced Crackers

Savoury snack crackers dotted with fennel seed. Your hostess will be delighted to receive this as part of a wine and cheese gift basket.

All-purpose flour	1 cup	250 mL
Instant yeast	1 tsp.	5 mL
Ground cumin	1/2 tsp.	2 mL
Ground coriander	1/2 tsp.	2 mL
Salt	1/2 tsp.	2 mL
Fennel seed	1/4 tsp.	1 mL
Cayenne pepper	1/8 tsp.	0.5 mL
Very warm water	6 tbsp.	100 mL
Olive (or cooking) oil	1 tbsp.	15 mL
Egg white (large)	1	1
Water	2 tbsp.	30 mL
Seasoned salt, sprinkle (optional)		

Combine first 7 ingredients in large bowl. Make a well in centre.

Add first amount of water and olive oil to well. Mix until soft dough forms. Turn out onto lightly floured surface. Knead for 5 to 10 minutes until smooth and elastic. Place in greased large bowl, turning once to grease top. Cover with greased waxed paper and tea towel. Let stand in oven with light on and door closed for 30 to 40 minutes until doubled in bulk. Punch dough down. Turn out onto lightly floured surface. Knead for about 1 minute until smooth. Roll out dough to 10 x 14 inch (25 x 35 cm) rectangle. Cut crosswise with pizza cutter into seven 2 inch (5 cm) strips. Arrange about 2 inches (5 cm) apart on greased baking sheets.

Beat egg white and second amount of water with fork in small cup. Brush evenly on each strip.

Sprinkle each strip with seasoned salt. Randomly poke several holes with fork in each strip to prevent air bubbles. Bake in 400°F (205°C) oven for about 5 minutes until golden. Remove from oven. Turn strips over. Bake in 350°F (175°C) oven for about 8 minutes until dry and crisp. Let stand on baking sheets for 5 minutes before transferring to cutting board. Cut each strip with serrated knife into 5 squares. Cut each square in half diagonally. Transfer to wire racks to cool. Makes about 6 dozen (72) crackers.

1 cracker: 9 Calories; 0.2 g Total Fat (0.2 g Mono, 0 g Poly, 0 g Sat); 0 mg Cholesterol; 1 g Carbohydrate; trace Fibre; 0 g Protein; 18 mg Sodium

Pictured on page 107.

Top Left: Pita Scoops, this page
Top Centre: Fiesta Relish, page 85
Top Right: Spiced Crackers, above
Bottom: Tijuana Triangles, this page

Gouda Chive Crackers

As "goud-as" or better than any store-bought cracker—and that's no "chive talkin'!" This generous recipe makes lots to give away.

All-purpose flour	2 cups	500 mL
Dried chives	2 tbsp.	30 mL
Envelope of instant yeast (or 2 1/4 tsp., 11 mL)	1/4 oz.	8 g
Salt	1/2 tsp.	2 mL
Very warm water	3/4 cup	175 mL
Olive (or cooking) oil	2 tbsp.	30 mL
Grated Gouda cheese	3/4 cup	175 mL
Egg white (large)	1	1
Water	2 tbsp.	30 mL
Freshly ground pepper, for garnish		

Combine first 4 ingredients in large bowl. Make a well in centre.

Add first amount of water and olive oil to well. Mix until soft dough forms. Turn out onto lightly floured surface. Knead for 5 to 10 minutes until smooth and elastic. Shape dough into ball. Flatten slightly.

Sprinkle with cheese. Press down lightly. Fold dough in half to enclose cheese. Knead for 1 to 2 minutes until evenly distributed. Place in greased large bowl, turning once to grease top. Cover with greased waxed paper and tea towel. Let stand in oven with light on and door closed for about 45 minutes until doubled in bulk. Punch dough down. Turn out onto lightly floured surface. Knead for about 1 minute until smooth. Divide dough in half. Roll out 1 half to 10 x 14 inch (25 x 35 cm) rectangle. Cover remaining half to prevent drying. Cut rectangle crosswise with pizza cutter into 2 inch (2.5 cm) strips. Arrange about 2 inches (5 cm) apart on greased baking sheets.

Beat egg white and second amount of water with fork in small cup. Brush evenly on each strip.

Garnish each strip with pepper. Randomly poke several holes with fork in each strip to prevent air bubbles. Bake in 400°F (205°C) oven for about 5 minutes until golden. Remove from oven. Turn strips over. Bake in 350°F (175°C) oven for 5 to 10 minutes until dry and crisp. Let stand on baking sheets for 5 minutes before transferring to cutting board. Cut each strip with serrated knife into 5 squares. Cut each square in half diagonally. Transfer to wire racks to cool. Cool baking sheets between batches. Repeat with remaining half of dough. Makes about 11 1/2 dozen (138) crackers.

1 cracker: 13 Calories; 0.4 g Total Fat (0.2 g Mono, 0 g Poly, 0.2 g Sat); 1 mg Cholesterol; 2 g Carbohydrate; trace Fibre; 0 g Protein; 15 mg Sodium

Pictured on page 109.

Cheese Puffs

Perfectly peppery—these are pretty in a festive Christmas tin. They won't be able to eat just one!

All-purpose flour	1 cup	250 mL
Icing (confectioner's) sugar	1/4 cup	60 mL
Cayenne pepper	1/8 tsp.	0.5 mL
Salt	1/8 tsp.	0.5 mL
Cold hard margarine (or butter), cut up	1/2 cup	125 mL
Grated sharp Cheddar cheese	3/4 cup	175 mL
Vanilla	1/2 tsp.	2 mL

Combine first 4 ingredients in large bowl. Cut in margarine until mixture resembles coarse crumbs.

Add cheese and vanilla. Mix well. Roll into 1 inch (2.5 cm) balls. Arrange about 1 inch (2.5 cm) apart on ungreased baking sheets. Bake in 350°F (175°C) oven for about 20 minutes until golden. Let stand on baking sheets for 5 minutes before removing to wire racks to cool. Makes about 2 dozen (24) cheese puffs.

1 cheese puff: 76 Calories; 5.3 g Total Fat (3 g Mono, 0.5 g Poly, 1.6 g Sat); 4 mg Cholesterol; 6 g Carbohydrate; trace Fibre; 2 g Protein; 83 mg Sodium

Pictured on page 109.

MEXICAN CHEESE PUFFS: Omit Cheddar cheese. Use same amount of grated Monterey Jack With Jalapeño cheese.

ITALIAN CHEESE PUFFS: Omit Cheddar cheese. Use same amount of grated Romano or Parmesan cheese.

Top Left and Bottom Left: Gouda Chive Crackers, this page
Centre Right: Cheese Puffs, this page

Wheat And Walnut Crackers

These earthy whole wheat crackers are an excellent choice to give in a small basket with Tapenade Salsa, page 82. A great gift for any hostess!

Whole wheat flour	1 1/2 cups	375 mL
Ground walnuts	3/4 cup	175 mL
Salt	1/4 tsp.	1 mL
Granulated sugar, just a pinch		
Water	1/2 cup	125 mL
Cooking oil	1 tbsp.	15 mL
Cooking oil	1 tbsp.	15 mL
Salt, sprinkle		

Combine first 4 ingredients in large bowl. Make a well in centre.

Add water and first amount of cooking oil to well. Stir until just moistened. Turn out onto lightly floured surface. Knead 6 times. Cover. Let stand for 15 minutes. Divide dough into 3 equal portions. Roll out 1 portion on lightly floured surface to 8 × 10 inch (20 × 25 cm) rectangle. Cover remaining portions to prevent drying.

Brush 1 tsp. (5 mL) of second amount of cooking oil evenly over rectangle. Sprinkle with salt. Cut with pizza cutter into 2 inch (5 cm) squares. Arrange about 1 inch (2.5 cm) apart on greased baking sheets. Bake in 375°F (190°C) oven for 5 minutes. Remove from oven. Turn squares over. Bake for another 5 to 8 minutes until edges are golden. Let stand on baking sheets for 5 minutes before removing to wire racks to cool. Repeat with remaining portions of dough. Cool baking sheets between batches. Makes about 5 dozen (60) crackers.

1 cracker: 21 Calories; 1.1 g Total Fat (0.4 g Mono, 0.6 g Poly, 0.1 g Sat);
    0 mg Cholesterol; 2 g Carbohydrate; trace Fibre; 1 g Protein; 10 mg Sodium

Pictured on page 83 and on back cover.

Cajun Crisps

A creatively crispy alternative to crackers. Bundle with some cheese or a dip for a spicy gift.

Large bagels (see Note)	2	2
Hard margarine (or butter), melted	1/4 cup	60 mL
Chili powder	2 tsp.	10 mL
Dried whole oregano	1/2 tsp.	2 mL
Dried basil	1/2 tsp.	2 mL
Garlic powder	1/2 tsp.	2 mL
Onion powder	1/2 tsp.	2 mL
Cayenne pepper	1/4 tsp.	1 mL
Grated Parmesan cheese	2 tbsp.	30 mL

Cut bagels in half crosswise. Cut each half into 1/8 inch (3 mm) half-moon slices. Arrange in single layer on greased baking sheets.

Combine next 7 ingredients in small bowl. Brush 1 side of slices with 1/2 of margarine mixture. Turn slices over. Brush opposite side of slices with remaining margarine mixture.

Sprinkle Parmesan cheese on each slice. Bake in 400°F (205°C) oven for 10 to 12 minutes until golden. Cool. Makes about 2 1/2 dozen (30) crisps.

1 crisp: 34 Calories; 1.9 g Total Fat (1.1 g Mono, 0.2 g Poly, 0.4 g Sat);
    0 mg Cholesterol; 3 g Carbohydrate; trace Fibre; 1 g Protein; 60 mg Sodium

Pictured on page 111.

Note: Use bagels with your favourite savoury flavour. Onion, herb, and whole wheat are good choices for these crisps.

Cheese And Walnut Rounds

A flavourful, melt-in-your-mouth snack. Great in a gift basket with some fresh fruit, wine and cheese.

Hard margarine (or butter), softened	1/2 cup	125 mL
Granulated sugar	1 tbsp.	15 mL
Large egg, fork-beaten	1	1
Salt	1/4 tsp.	1 mL
Coarse ground pepper	1/4 tsp.	1 mL
All-purpose flour	1 cup	250 mL
Grated Parmesan cheese	1/4 cup	60 mL
Finely chopped walnuts, toasted (see Tip, page 22)	3 tbsp.	50 mL
Egg white (large), fork-beaten	1	1
Grated Parmesan cheese	4 tsp.	20 mL
Finely chopped walnuts, toasted (see Tip, page 22)	1 tbsp.	15 mL

Cream margarine and sugar in medium bowl. Add egg, salt and pepper. Beat well.

Combine flour and first amounts of Parmesan cheese and walnuts in small bowl. Add to margarine mixture. Mix until no dry flour remains. Roll into 8 inch (20 cm) long log. Wrap with plastic wrap. Chill for about 2 hours until firm. Discard plastic wrap. Cut log into 1/4 inch (6 mm) slices. Arrange about 1 inch (2.5 cm) apart on ungreased baking sheets.

Brush 1 side of each slice with egg white.

Combine second amounts of Parmesan cheese and walnuts in small cup. Sprinkle on each slice. Bake in 400°F (205°C) oven for about 12 minutes until edges are golden. Let stand on baking sheets for 5 minutes before removing to wire racks to cool. Makes about 2 1/2 dozen (30) rounds.

1 round: 61 Calories; 4.4 g Total Fat (2.4 g Mono, 0.8 g Poly, 1 g Sat); 8 mg Cholesterol; 4 g Carbohydrate; trace Fibre; 2 g Protein; 83 mg Sodium

Pictured below.

Left: Cheese And Walnut Rounds, above

Right: Cajun Crisps, page 110

Chili-Jack Biscotti

A spicy biscotti flecked with jalapeño. Makes a tasty gift packaged with Calico Bean Soup Mix, page 52.

All-purpose flour	2 1/4 cups	550 mL
Grated Monterey Jack With Jalapeño cheese	1/2 cup	125 mL
Baking powder	1 tsp.	5 mL
Salt	1/2 tsp.	2 mL
Large eggs	2	2
Cooking oil	1/3 cup	75 mL
Frozen kernel corn, thawed and chopped	1/2 cup	125 mL
Can of diced green chilies, drained and blotted dry	4 oz.	113 g
Chili powder	1 tsp.	5 mL
Paprika	1 tsp.	5 mL
Salt, just a pinch		

Combine first 4 ingredients in large bowl. Make a well in centre. Set aside.

Beat eggs and cooking oil with fork in small bowl.

Add corn and chilies. Beat well. Add mixture to well. Mix until stiff dough forms. Turn out onto lightly floured surface. Knead 6 times. Divide dough in half. Roll each half into 6 inch (15 cm) long log. Place about 2 inches (5 cm) apart on greased baking sheet. Flatten each log slightly.

Combine chili powder, paprika and second amount of salt in small cup. Sprinkle on both logs. Bake in 350°F (175°C) oven for 25 to 30 minutes until golden. Let stand on baking sheet for about 20 minutes until cool enough to handle. Cut each log diagonally with serrated knife into 1/2 inch (12 mm) slices. Arrange evenly spaced apart on same baking sheet. Bake in 275°F (140°C) oven for 50 minutes, turning once at halftime. Turn oven off. Let stand overnight in oven with door closed until dry and crisp. Makes about 1 1/2 dozen (18) biscotti.

1 biscotti: 125 Calories; 6.1 g Total Fat (3 g Mono, 1.5 g Poly, 1.1 g Sat); 27 mg Cholesterol; 14 g Carbohydrate; 1 g Fibre; 3 g Protein; 114 mg Sodium

Pictured on page 83.

Cornmeal Pesto Biscotti

Wrap these in cellophane and present in an Italian gift basket, page 182, with Mushroom Risotto Mix, page 48. Irresistible!

All-purpose flour	1 3/4 cups	425 mL
Grated Romano cheese	1/2 cup	125 mL
Yellow cornmeal	1/3 cup	75 mL
Shelled pumpkin seeds	3 tbsp.	50 mL
Granulated sugar	2 tsp.	10 mL
Baking powder	1/2 tsp.	2 mL
Large eggs	3	3
Basil pesto	1/4 cup	60 mL
Large egg, fork-beaten	1	1
Coarse sea salt	1/8 tsp.	0.5 mL

Combine first 6 ingredients in large bowl. Make a well in centre.

Beat first amount of eggs and pesto with fork in small bowl. Add to well. Mix until stiff dough forms. Turn out onto lightly floured surface. Knead 6 times. Roll into 12 inch (30 cm) long log. Place on greased baking sheet. Flatten slightly.

Brush dough evenly with second amount of egg. Sprinkle with salt. Bake in 350°F (175°C) oven for 25 to 30 minutes until golden. Let stand on baking sheet for about 20 minutes until cool enough to handle. Cut log diagonally with serrated knife into 1/2 inch (12 mm) slices. Arrange evenly spaced apart on same baking sheet. Bake in 350°F (175°C) oven for about 20 minutes, turning slices at halftime, until dry and crisp. Let stand on baking sheet for 5 minutes before removing to wire rack to cool. Makes about 1 1/2 dozen (18) biscotti.

1 biscotti: 103 Calories; 3.8 g Total Fat (1.6 g Mono, 0.6 g Poly, 1.1 g Sat); 51 mg Cholesterol; 13 g Carbohydrate; 1 g Fibre; 4 g Protein; 77 mg Sodium

Pictured on page 113 and on page 182.

Top Right: Cornmeal Pesto Biscotti, above
Bottom Left: Apricot Nut Wafers, page 114

Herb And Spice Nuts, below, in Window Gift Bag, page 163

Herb And Spice Nuts

There's just a bit of heat in this rosemary-scented nut mix.
A spicy gift to bring to any party.

Raw cashews	1 1/2 cups	375 mL
Raw macadamia nuts	1 cup	250 mL
Whole natural almonds	1 cup	250 mL
Brown sugar, packed	1/3 cup	75 mL
Dried crushed chilies	2 tsp.	10 mL
Dried rosemary, crushed	2 tsp.	10 mL
Salt	1 tsp.	5 mL
Pepper	1/2 tsp.	2 mL
Egg white (large)	1	1

Combine first 8 ingredients in large bowl.

Beat egg white with fork in small cup. Add to nut mixture. Stir until nuts are coated. Spread evenly in greased baking sheet with sides. Bake in 350°F (175°C) oven for about 20 minutes, stirring occasionally, until golden. Makes about 4 cups (1 L).

1/4 cup (60 mL): 216 Calories; 17.8 g Total Fat (12 g Mono, 2.2 g Poly, 2.7 g Sat); 0 mg Cholesterol; 13 g Carbohydrate; 2 g Fibre; 5 g Protein; 161 mg Sodium

Pictured above.

Apricot Nut Wafers

A sprinkling of pepper perfectly accentuates gently sweet apricot in these crispy wafers. Add a small jar of cream cheese spread or jam for a wonderful home-baked gift.

All-purpose flour	3/4 cup	175 mL
Baking soda	1/4 tsp.	1 mL
Salt	1/4 tsp.	1 mL
Pepper	1/8 tsp.	0.5 mL
Cold hard margarine (or butter), cut up	2 tbsp.	30 mL
Finely chopped pecans, toasted (see Tip, page 22)	3 tbsp.	50 mL
Finely chopped dried apricot	3 tbsp.	50 mL
Milk	1/4 cup	60 mL
Cooking oil	1 1/2 tsp.	7 mL
Salt, sprinkle		
Pepper, sprinkle		

Combine first 4 ingredients in medium bowl. Cut in margarine until mixture resembles coarse crumbs.

Add pecans and apricot. Stir. Make a well in centre.

Add milk to well. Stir until just moistened. Turn out onto lightly floured surface. Knead 6 times. Divide dough in half. Roll out 1 half to 4 x 10 inch (10 x 25 cm) rectangle. Cover remaining half to prevent drying.

Brush rectangle with 1/2 of cooking oil. Sprinkle with salt and pepper. Cut with pizza cutter into 1 x 2 inch (2.5 x 5 cm) rectangles. Arrange about 1 inch (2.5 cm) apart on greased baking sheets. Bake in 375°F (190°C) oven for 6 to 8 minutes until golden. Remove from oven. Turn wafers over. Bake for another 6 to 8 minutes until dry and crisp. Let stand on baking sheets for 5 minutes before removing to wire racks to cool. Repeat with remaining half of dough. Cool baking sheets between batches. Makes about 3 1/2 dozen (42) wafers.

1 wafer: 22 Calories; 1.2 g Total Fat (0.7 g Mono, 0.2 g Poly, 0.2 g Sat); 0 mg Cholesterol; 2 g Carbohydrate; trace Fibre; 0 g Protein; 31 mg Sodium

Pictured on page 113.

Left: Cranberry Cheese Muffins, page 116

Right: Zucchini Parmesan Pots, this page

Zucchini Parmesan Pots

Baking breads in clay pots creates an appetizing and attractive gift. After the loaves cool, return to pots and wrap them individually in colourful cellophane.

Clay pots (3 inch, 7.5 cm, diameter), see Note	6	6
All-purpose flour	3 cups	750 mL
Grated zucchini (with peel)	1 cup	250 mL
Grated Parmesan cheese	1/4 cup	60 mL
Granulated sugar	3 tbsp.	50 mL
Minced onion flakes	1 tbsp.	15 mL
Baking powder	1 tsp.	5 mL
Baking soda	1/2 tsp.	2 mL
Salt	1/2 tsp.	2 mL
Large eggs	2	2
Buttermilk (or reconstituted from powder)	1 cup	250 mL
Hard margarine (or butter), melted	1/3 cup	75 mL
Grated Parmesan cheese	2 tbsp.	30 mL

Soak clay pots in water for 30 minutes. Line bottom of each pot with waxed paper. Place on baking sheet.

Combine next 8 ingredients in large bowl. Make a well in centre.

Beat eggs with fork in medium bowl. Add buttermilk and margarine. Stir. Add to well. Stir until just moistened. Spoon batter into pots.

Sprinkle 1 tsp. (5 mL) Parmesan cheese over each. Bake in 350°F (175°C) oven for 30 to 35 minutes until wooden pick inserted in centre of loaf comes out clean. Let stand in pots for 10 minutes before removing to wire racks to cool. Makes 6 loaves. Each loaf cuts into 3 slices, for a total of 18 slices.

1 slice: 146 Calories; 5.1 g Total Fat (2.8 g Mono, 0.5 g Poly, 1.4 g Sat); 26 mg Cholesterol; 20 g Carbohydrate; 1 g Fibre; 5 g Protein; 227 mg Sodium

Pictured on page 104 and above.

Note: If preferred, batter may be divided among 6 greased 3/4 cup (175 mL) ramekins set on baking sheet. Bake as directed.

Cranberry Cheese Muffins

Great for breakfast! Everyone will love these tender muffins with tart cranberries and spicy cinnamon. Wrap in a cellophane bag and a bright Christmas tea towel for your next brunch invitation.

All-purpose flour	3 cups	750 mL
Grated sharp Cheddar cheese	1 1/2 cups	375 mL
Dried cranberries	1 cup	250 mL
Brown sugar, packed	3/4 cup	175 mL
Baking powder	1 tbsp.	15 mL
Ground cinnamon	1 tsp.	5 mL
Salt	1 tsp.	5 mL
Dried thyme	1/2 tsp.	2 mL
Large eggs	2	2
Milk	1 cup	250 mL
Cooking oil	1/3 cup	75 mL

Combine first 8 ingredients in large bowl. Make a well in centre.

Beat eggs, milk and cooking oil with whisk in medium bowl. Add to well. Stir until just moistened. Grease 12 muffin cups with cooking spray. Fill cups 3/4 full. Bake in 375°F (190°C) oven for 20 to 25 minutes until wooden pick inserted in centre of muffin comes out clean. Let stand in pan for 5 minutes before removing to wire rack to cool. Makes 12 muffins.

1 muffin: 331 Calories; 12.8 g Total Fat (5.6 g Mono, 2.3 g Poly, 4.1 g Sat); 52 mg Cholesterol; 45 g Carbohydrate; 2 g Fibre; 9 g Protein; 411 mg Sodium

Pictured on page 115.

Sesame Spice Triangles

Crispy crackers with a touch of Asian flavour. Have several cellophane bags of these on hand to give to guests as a thank you for coming to dinner.

Hard margarine (or butter), softened	1/2 cup	125 mL
Brown sugar, packed	1/2 cup	125 mL
Large egg	1	1
Whole wheat flour	1 cup	250 mL
All-purpose flour	1 cup	250 mL
Sesame seeds, toasted (see Tip, page 22)	3 tbsp.	50 mL
Poppy seeds	2 tbsp.	30 mL
Ground ginger	2 tsp.	10 mL
Chinese five-spice powder	1 tsp.	5 mL
Baking soda	1/2 tsp.	2 mL
Salt	1/4 tsp.	1 mL
Soy sauce	1/2 tbsp.	7 mL

Cream margarine and brown sugar in large bowl. Add egg. Beat well.

Combine next 8 ingredients in medium bowl. Add to margarine mixture. Beat until well combined. Mixture will be crumbly. Shape into ball. Flatten into disc. Wrap with plastic wrap. Chill for 1 hour. Discard plastic wrap. Roll out dough between 2 sheets of waxed paper to 12 inch (30 cm) square. Discard top sheet of waxed paper.

Brush soy sauce evenly on dough. Cut with pizza cutter into 2 inch (5 cm) squares. Cut each square in half diagonally. Arrange about 1 inch (2.5 cm) apart on greased baking sheets. Bake in 350°F (175°C) oven for about 10 minutes until golden. Let stand on baking sheets for 5 minutes before removing to wire racks to cool. Makes about 6 dozen (72) triangles.

1 triangle: 35 Calories; 1.8 g Total Fat (1 g Mono, 0.3 g Poly, 0.4 g Sat); 3 mg Cholesterol; 4 g Carbohydrate; trace Fibre; 1 g Protein; 42 mg Sodium

Pictured on page 117.

Left: Sesame Soy Walnuts, below

Right: Sesame Spice Triangles, page 116

Sesame Soy Walnuts

Why should you make these crisp snacks for Christmas?
Why "nut?" Great to bring to your next Christmas party.

Low-sodium soy sauce	1/3 cup	75 mL
Granulated sugar	3 tbsp.	50 mL
Sesame oil, for flavour	1 tsp.	5 mL
Ground ginger	1 tsp.	5 mL
Ground allspice	1/4 tsp.	1 mL
Walnut halves	6 cups	1.5 L
Sesame seeds	1/3 cup	75 mL

Combine first 5 ingredients in large bowl.

Add walnuts and sesame seeds. Stir until coated. Spread evenly in parchment paper-lined baking sheet with sides. Bake in 250°F (120°C) oven for 40 to 45 minutes, stirring occasionally, until golden. Cool. Store in airtight container for up to 1 month. Makes about 6 1/2 cups (1.6 L).

1/4 cup (60 mL): 177 Calories; 16.4 g Total Fat (3.9 g Mono, 10.1 g Poly, 1.5 g Sat); 0 mg Cholesterol; 6 g Carbohydrate; 1 g Fibre; 4 g Protein; 108 mg Sodium

Pictured above.

Sweet Treats

During the Christmas season we look forward to indulging in those sweet treats we love so much. Who wouldn't be thrilled to receive a delicate package of truffles, rich fudge or smooth chocolate bark?

Recipes for fudge and squares can be prepared as early as two months ahead. Cut them up, freeze them in airtight containers between layers of waxed paper, and pull them out when you're ready to put together your gift. Mix and match these

treats in decorative tins or holiday candy dishes wrapped in colourful cellophane. Remember, adding a label that offers a "best-before" date (three weeks after giving) will ensure they'll be enjoyed at their freshest.

These confections are also great for small gift packages, and individually wrapped clusters of mint candies or nutty brittle can make a festive accent to your dinner table.

Chocolate Almond Fudge

Dark, smooth, sweet—and loaded with almonds.
Everyone will love receiving this at Christmas!

Miniature marshmallows	9 cups	2.25 L
Granulated sugar	2 cups	500 mL
Small can of evaporated milk	5 1/2 oz.	160 mL
Hard margarine (or butter)	1/2 cup	125 mL
Salt, just a pinch		
Dark chocolate bars (3 1/2 oz., 100 g, each), chopped	3	3
Almond flavouring	1 tsp.	5 mL
Slivered almonds, toasted (see Tip, page 22)	2 1/2 cups	625 mL

Combine first 5 ingredients in large heavy saucepan. Bring to a rolling boil on medium, stirring often. Boil for 5 minutes, stirring constantly. Remove from heat.

Add chocolate and flavouring. Stir until smooth.

Add almonds. Mix well. Line 9 × 9 inch (22 × 22 cm) pan with foil, leaving 1 inch (2.5 cm) overhang on 2 sides. Grease foil with cooking spray. Spread almond mixture evenly in pan. Chill for about 3 hours until firm. Holding foil, remove fudge from pan. Discard foil. Cuts into 64 pieces.

1 piece: 118 Calories; 5.9 g Total Fat (3.3 g Mono, 0.8 g Poly, 1.5 g Sat); 1 mg Cholesterol; 16 g Carbohydrate; 1 g Fibre; 2 g Protein; 25 mg Sodium

Pictured below.

Left and Bottom Centre: Chocolate Almond Fudge, above

Right: Cashew Buttercrunch, page 120

Cashew Buttercrunch

Don't let anyone "ca-shew" nibbling on this, or they'll all want some. Wrap it up quickly in a festive mug or a Good Neighbour gift basket, page 184.

Butter (not margarine)	1 cup	250 mL
Granulated sugar	1 cup	250 mL
White corn syrup	2 tbsp.	30 mL
Water	2 tbsp.	30 mL
Coarsely chopped salted cashews	1 cup	250 mL
Vanilla	1 tsp.	5 mL
Milk chocolate chips	1 cup	250 mL
Coarsely chopped salted cashews	2/3 cup	150 mL

Heat and stir first 4 ingredients in large heavy saucepan on medium for about 10 minutes until boiling and sugar is dissolved. Boil gently, uncovered, for about 15 minutes, brushing side of saucepan with wet pastry brush to dissolve any sugar crystals, until mixture is golden brown and small spoonful dropped in ice water is hard and brittle when pressed together. Remove from heat.

Carefully add first amount of cashews and vanilla. Mixture might sputter. Stir well. Line 9 x 13 inch (22 x 33 cm) pan with foil, leaving 1 inch (2.5 cm) overhang on 2 sides. Grease foil with cooking spray. Spread cashew mixture evenly in pan.

Sprinkle chocolate chips over top. Let stand for about 5 minutes until softened. Spread evenly over cashew mixture.

Immediately sprinkle with second amount of cashews. Cool. Holding foil, remove buttercrunch from pan. Discard foil. Break buttercrunch into irregular-shaped pieces, about 2 x 2 inches (5 x 5 cm) each. Makes about 24 pieces.

1 piece: 207 Calories; 15 g Total Fat (5.8 g Mono, 1.2 g Poly, 7.3 g Sat); 24 mg Cholesterol; 18 g Carbohydrate; trace Fibre; 2 g Protein; 155 mg Sodium

Pictured on front cover, on page 119 and on page 184.

Oriental Crunch

Caramel corn with an Oriental twist. Send it in a College Care Package, page 176, to someone who needs a taste of home. Or put it in festive bags to give as favours at your dinner party.

Popped corn (about 1/4 cup, 60 mL, unpopped)	6 cups	1.5 L
Dry chow mein noodles	2 cups	500 mL
Brown sugar, packed	1/2 cup	125 mL
Hard margarine (or butter)	1/4 cup	60 mL
Golden corn syrup	2 tbsp.	30 mL
Fancy (mild) molasses	1 tbsp.	15 mL
Chinese five-spice powder	1 tsp.	5 mL
Salt	1/4 tsp.	1 mL
Baking soda	1/4 tsp.	1 mL
Sesame seeds, toasted (see Tip, page 22)	1/4 cup	60 mL

Combine popped corn and chow mein noodles in extra-large bowl. Set aside.

Heat and stir next 6 ingredients in small heavy saucepan on medium for about 5 minutes until boiling and brown sugar is dissolved. Reduce heat to medium-low. Simmer, uncovered, for 3 minutes, stirring constantly. Remove from heat.

Add baking soda. Stir well. Pour over popped corn mixture.

Sprinkle with sesame seeds. Stir with wooden spoon until popped corn mixture is coated. Spread evenly in greased baking sheet with sides. Bake in 250°F (120°C) oven for 30 minutes. Remove from oven. Loosen mixture with spatula. Cool. Break into bite-size pieces. Store in airtight container for up to 1 month. Makes about 9 1/2 cups (2.4 L).

1/4 cup (60 mL): 51 Calories; 2.6 g Total Fat (1.2 g Mono, 0.8 g Poly, 0.5 g Sat); 0 mg Cholesterol; 7 g Carbohydrate; trace Fibre; 1 g Protein; 54 mg Sodium

Pictured on page 121 and on page 176.

Centre Right: Oriental Crunch, above
Top Right and Bottom Left: Candied Cashew Popcorn, page 122

Candied Cashew Popcorn

A great gift idea for your children's teachers. Fill decorative cellophane bags and tie each with a fancy ribbon.

Popped corn (about 2/3 cup, 150 mL, unpopped)	16 cups	4 L
Granulated sugar	3 cups	750 mL
Water	2/3 cup	150 mL
Hard margarine (or butter)	1/3 cup	75 mL
Vanilla	1 tsp.	5 mL
Salt	1/4 tsp.	1 mL
Raw cashews, toasted (see Tip, page 22)	2 1/2 cups	625 mL

Measure popped corn into greased large roasting pan. Set aside.

Heat and stir next 4 ingredients in heavy medium saucepan on medium for about 10 minutes until boiling and sugar is dissolved. Boil gently, uncovered, for 25 to 35 minutes, without stirring, brushing side of saucepan with wet pastry brush to dissolve any sugar crystals, until golden brown. Remove from heat.

Add salt. Stir well. Pour over popped corn.

Add cashews. Stir with wooden spoon until popped corn mixture is coated. Divide and spread evenly in 2 greased baking sheets with sides. Cool. Break into bite-size pieces. Store at room temperature in airtight container for up to 1 month. Makes about 20 cups (5 L).

1 cup (250 mL): 282 Calories; 11.9 g Total Fat (7.1 g Mono, 1.9 g Poly, 2.4 g Sat); 0 mg Cholesterol; 43 g Carbohydrate; 1 g Fibre; 4 g Protein; 71 mg Sodium

Pictured on page 121.

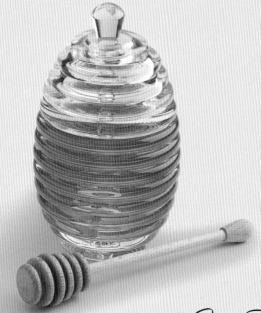

Dipped Sugar Plums

When the kids are tucked snugly in their beds, make these sugar plums. For pretty table favours, pack these in pairs in small candy boxes topped with a ribbon.

Shelled pistachios	1/2 cup	125 mL
Chopped crystallized ginger	2 tbsp.	30 mL
Grated orange zest	1 tsp.	5 mL
Liquid honey	1 tbsp.	15 mL
Whole pitted dessert dates (see Note)	28	28
Semi-sweet chocolate baking squares (1 oz., 28 g, each), coarsely chopped	7	7
Finely chopped pistachios	1/3 cup	75 mL

Put first 3 ingredients into blender or food processor. Pulse with on/off motion, scraping down sides if necessary, until very finely chopped. Transfer to small bowl.

Add honey. Stir until paste consistency.

Cut dates almost in half lengthwise. Gently spread 1/2 tsp. (2 mL) pistachio mixture on 1 half of each date. Press halves together to enclose mixture.

Heat chocolate in small heavy saucepan on lowest heat, stirring often, until almost melted. Do not overheat. Remove from heat. Stir until smooth. Transfer to custard cup. Holding 1 stuffed date by end, dip straight down into chocolate until coated halfway.

Immediately press chocolate-coated end in second amount of pistachios in small shallow dish until coated. Place on waxed paper-lined baking sheet. Repeat with remaining stuffed dates, chocolate and pistachios. Chill until set. Makes 28 sugar plums.

1 sugar plum: 84 Calories; 4.3 g Total Fat (2.1 g Mono, 0.4 g Poly, 1.5 g Sat); 0 mg Cholesterol; 13 g Carbohydrate; 1 g Fibre; 1 g Protein; 2 mg Sodium

Pictured on page 123.

Note: Choose smooth, shiny, plump dates from the bulk section of your grocery store.

Dipped Sugar Plums, above

Party Mints

Cool, creamy and colourful—sure to be a hit. Add as much food colouring as desired to make softer or bolder shades. Fill a whimsical candy dish or Woven Treasure Tin, this page, with these minty morsels for a cheerful hostess gift.

Block of cream cheese, softened	4 oz.	125 g
Icing (confectioner's) sugar	3 1/3 cups	825 mL

COOL MINTS
Peppermint flavouring	1/4 tsp.	1 mL
Green liquid (or paste) food colouring		

LEMON MINTS
Lemon flavouring	1/8 tsp.	0.5 mL
Peppermint flavouring	1/8 tsp.	0.5 mL
Yellow liquid (or paste) food colouring		

ORANGE MINTS
Orange flavouring	1/8 tsp.	0.5 mL
Peppermint flavouring	1/8 tsp.	0.5 mL
Yellow liquid (or paste) food colouring		
Red liquid (or paste) food colouring		

CHERRY MINTS
Cherry flavouring	1/8 tsp.	0.5 mL
Peppermint flavouring	1/8 tsp.	0.5 mL
Red liquid (or paste food colouring)		

BUTTER MINTS
Butter flavouring	1/8 tsp.	0.5 mL
Peppermint flavouring	1/8 tsp.	0.5 mL
Yellow liquid (or paste) food colouring		

Beat cream cheese with 1 cup (250 mL) icing sugar in medium bowl until smooth.

Add remaining icing sugar in 2 additions, beating well after each addition, until smooth. Turn out onto icing sugar-coated surface. Knead for about 1 minute until smooth, adding more icing sugar if necessary to prevent sticking. Divide into 4 portions. Dent each portion with thumb.

Add 1 of the suggested flavour/colour combinations to each dent to make an assortment of mints. Knead each portion on icing sugar-coated surface until colour is even. Divide each portion into 4 equal pieces. Roll each piece into 1/2 inch (12 mm) diameter rope. Cover remaining portions to prevent drying. Cut each rope into 1/2 inch (12 mm) slices. Place on waxed paper-lined baking sheets. Let stand overnight until dry. Makes about 26 1/2 dozen (318) mints.

1 mint: 7 Calories; 0.1 g Total Fat (0 g Mono, 0 g Poly, 0.1 g Sat); 0 mg Cholesterol; 1 g Carbohydrate; 0 g Fibre; 0 g Protein; 1 mg Sodium

Pictured on page 125.

✷ Woven Treasure Tin ✷

Clean tin cans are perfect for packaging small amounts of sweets or snacks. This tin, embellished with ribbons woven in a decorative pattern, is ideal for giving candy and confections. Or, you can add a quick coat of paint and some glitter to transform any tin into a festive container.

MATERIALS
Tin can (19 oz., 540 mL, size)
Peel-and-stick felt piece (9 x 12 inches, 22 x 30 cm)
Ribbon (1/2 inch, 12 mm, width)
Ribbon (1 inch, 2.5 cm, width)
Metallic bead trim

TOOLS
pencil, scissors, measuring tape, glue gun

Trace the bottom of the tin can on the backing of the felt and cut out the circle.

Measure the height of the tin and add 1 inch (2.5 cm). Cut 7 pieces of each ribbon to this measurement. Glue the end of each ribbon to the top edge of the tin, alternating colours (see picture).

Measure the circumference of the tin and add 1/2 inch (12 mm). Cut 3 pieces of the 1/2 inch (12 mm) ribbon and 2 pieces of the 1 inch (2.5 cm) ribbon to this measurement.

Glue 1 end of one 1 inch (2.5 cm) ribbon horizontally, just under the top edge of the tin (see picture). Weave the ribbon around the tin, over and under the vertical ribbons, securing the end to the tin with glue. Continue gluing and weaving, alternating colours, until you reach the bottom of the tin. Glue the vertical ribbon ends to the bottom of the tin. Remove the backing from the felt circle. Secure the felt to the bottom of the tin. Glue the metallic bead trim around the top edge of the tin to finish.

Pictured on page 125.

Left: Orange Party Mints, this page
Top Centre: Cool Party Mints and Cherry Party Mints, this page
Right: Lemon Party Mints, this page, in Woven Treasure Tin, above

Birdseed Brittle

*A sweet, crunchy gift to bring and
share with your co-workers...*

*"Flockin' around the Christmas tree,
at your office party hop.
Flockin' around the Christmas tree,
eatin' candy and talkin' shop!"*

Butter (not margarine), softened	1/4 cup	60 mL
Brown sugar, packed	1/2 cup	125 mL
Golden corn syrup	1/3 cup	75 mL
All-purpose flour	1/2 cup	125 mL
Unsalted roasted shelled sunflower seeds	1/4 cup	60 mL
Shelled pumpkin seeds	1/4 cup	60 mL
Sesame seeds, toasted (see Tip, page 22)	2 tbsp.	30 mL
Flaxseed	2 tbsp.	30 mL

Cream butter and brown sugar in medium bowl. Add corn
syrup. Beat well. Add flour. Mix well.

Add remaining 4 ingredients. Mix well. Roll out evenly
between 2 sheets of parchment paper to 11 x 17 inch
(28 x 43 cm) rectangle. Transfer parchment paper with seed
mixture to 11 x 17 inch (28 x 43 cm) baking sheet with sides.
Chill for 10 minutes. Discard top sheet of parchment paper.
Bake in 400°F (205°C) oven for 5 to 10 minutes until golden.
Let stand on baking sheet for 10 minutes before removing
parchment paper with seed mixture to wire rack to cool.
Break brittle into irregular-shaped pieces, about 2 x 2 inches
(5 x 5 cm) each. Makes about 40 pieces.

1 piece: 51 Calories; 2.5 g Total Fat (0.7 g Mono, 0.8 g Poly, 0.9 g Sat);
3 mg Cholesterol; 7 g Carbohydrate; trace Fibre; 1 g Protein; 18 mg Sodium

Pictured on page 127.

Cashew Pecan Praline

*Pack this attractive candy in a decorative ceramic container
or cellophane bag and give to someone with a sweet tooth.
When processed to a fine powder, praline is wonderful
sprinkled on a frosted cake, ice cream or pudding.*

Raw cashews	1 1/2 cups	375 mL
Pecan halves	1 1/2 cups	375 mL
Granulated sugar	3 cups	750 mL
Water	3/4 cup	175 mL

Spread cashews and pecans evenly in ungreased shallow pan.
Bake in 350°F (175°C) oven for 5 to 10 minutes, stirring or
shaking often, until just toasted. Turn oven off. Let stand in
pan in oven to keep warm.

Heat and stir sugar and water in medium saucepan on
medium-high for about 5 minutes until boiling and sugar
is dissolved. Boil, uncovered, without stirring, for about
10 minutes, brushing side of saucepan with wet pastry brush
to dissolve any sugar crystals, until golden brown. Remove
from heat. Add nuts. Stir. Immediately pour into greased
10 x 15 inch (25 x 38 cm) jelly roll pan. Working quickly,
spread mixture evenly to sides of pan. Let stand in jelly roll
pan on wire rack for 1 to 2 hours until cooled. Break
praline into irregular-shaped pieces, about 1 1/2 x 4 inches
(3.8 x 10 cm) each. Store in airtight container for up to
8 weeks. Makes about 24 pieces.

1 piece: 202 Calories; 9 g Total Fat (5.5 g Mono, 1.9 g Poly, 1.2 g Sat);
0 mg Cholesterol; 31 g Carbohydrate; 1 g Fibre; 2 g Protein; 2 mg Sodium

Pictured on page 127.

CASHEW PECAN PRALINE TOPPING: Place 1 or 2 pieces of
praline in large resealable freezer bag. Seal. Hit with meat
mallet or hammer until finely crushed. Praline can also be
processed in blender to a fine powder. Sprinkle over cake,
ice cream, fruit salad, or fold into your favourite mousse
or pudding.

Left: Birdseed Brittle, this page
Right: Cashew Pecan Praline, above

White Chocolate Almond Fudge

Rich almond flavour and white chocolate make this fudge truly decadent. Perfect for when you need a number of small gifts. Set in coloured tissue and tulle in a small shallow gift box.

Miniature marshmallows	4 cups	1 L
Granulated sugar	1 1/2 cups	375 mL
Small can of evaporated milk (or half-and-half cream)	5 1/2 oz.	160 mL
Hard margarine (or butter)	2 tbsp.	30 mL
Salt	1/4 tsp.	1 mL
White chocolate chips	2 cups	500 mL
Vanilla	2 tsp.	10 mL
Coarsely chopped slivered almonds, toasted (see Tip, page 22)	1 1/2 cups	375 mL

Combine first 5 ingredients in large heavy saucepan. Bring to a rolling boil on medium, stirring often. Boil, uncovered, for 5 minutes, stirring constantly. Remove from heat.

Add white chocolate chips and vanilla. Stir until smooth.

Add almonds. Mix well. Line 9 x 9 inch (22 x 22 cm) pan with foil, leaving 1 inch (2.5 cm) overhang on 2 sides. Grease foil with cooking spray. Spread almond mixture evenly in pan. Chill for about 3 hours until firm. Holding foil, remove fudge from pan. Discard foil. Cuts into 64 pieces.

1 piece: 85 Calories; 4 g Total Fat (1.9 g Mono, 0.4 g Poly, 1.4 g Sat); 2 mg Cholesterol; 12 g Carbohydrate; trace Fibre; 1 g Protein; 23 mg Sodium

Pictured on page 130.

Friesens' Fudge

A melt-in-your-mouth chocolate and toffee fudge that's easy to make and a joy to give. Share some with a special friend in your life.

Miniature marshmallows	4 cups	1 L
Granulated sugar	1 1/2 cups	375 mL
Evaporated milk	2/3 cup	150 mL
Butter (or hard margarine)	1/4 cup	60 mL
Salt	1/4 tsp.	1 mL
Bag of milk (or semi-sweet) chocolate chips	10 1/2 oz.	300 g
Vanilla	1 tsp.	5 mL
Package of toffee bits (such as Chipits Skor Toffee Bits), see Note	8 oz.	225 g

Line 9 x 9 inch (22 x 22 cm) pan with foil, leaving 1 inch (2.5 cm) overhang on 2 sides. Grease foil with cooking spray. Set aside. Combine first 5 ingredients in large saucepan. Bring to a rolling boil, stirring often. Boil, uncovered, for 5 minutes, stirring constantly. Remove from heat.

Add chocolate chips and vanilla. Stir until smooth.

Add toffee bits. Stir well. Immediately pour into prepared pan. Smooth top. Let stand until cool. Holding foil, remove fudge from pan. Discard foil. Cuts into 64 pieces.

1 piece: 82 Calories; 3.6 g Total Fat (0.8 g Mono, 0.1 g Poly, 1.5 g Sat); 6 mg Cholesterol; 12 g Carbohydrate; trace Fibre; 1 g Protein; 33 mg Sodium

Pictured on page 130.

Note: Omit toffee bits. Use 4 crushed Skor or Heath chocolate bars. For best results, put unwrapped bars in a resealable freezer bag and freeze for 15 minutes. Seal bag. Hit with a meat mallet or hammer until bars are in small pieces.

Cherry Macadamia Fudge

This creamy milk chocolate fudge accented with a delicious pairing of cherries and toasted macadamia nuts makes a divinely different gift. Pack in small festive boxes or clear plastic containers and top with a gold ribbon.

Milk chocolate chips	2 cups	500 mL
Can of sweetened condensed milk	11 oz.	300 mL
Icing (confectioner's) sugar	1/2 cup	125 mL
Chopped raw macadamia nuts, toasted (see Tip, page 22)	3/4 cup	175 mL
Chopped dried cherries	1/2 cup	125 mL
Cherry-flavoured liqueur (such as Kirsch)	1 tsp.	5 mL

Heat chocolate chips in heavy medium saucepan on lowest heat, stirring often, until almost melted. Do not overheat. Remove from heat. Stir until smooth.

Add condensed milk and icing sugar. Stir until smooth.

Add macadamia nuts, cherries and liqueur. Mix well. Line 8 × 8 inch (20 × 20 cm) pan with foil, leaving 1 inch (2.5 cm) overhang on 2 sides. Grease foil with cooking spray. Spread cherry mixture evenly in pan. Chill for 3 to 4 hours until firm. Holding foil, remove fudge from pan. Discard foil. Cuts into 64 pieces.

1 piece: 67 Calories; 3.5 g Total Fat (1.7 g Mono, 0.1 g Poly, 1.6 g Sat);
   3 mg Cholesterol; 9 g Carbohydrate; trace Fibre; 1 g Protein; 12 mg Sodium

Pictured on page 131.

Almond Pistachio Fudge

An enticing sweet treat infused with exotic East Indian flavour. Cut into diamond shapes and wrap individually in cellophane and ribbon for party gifts or table favours.

Homogenized milk	1 1/2 cups	375 mL
Ground almonds, toasted (see Tip, page 22)	1 1/4 cups	300 mL
Granulated sugar	1 cup	250 mL
Medium unsweetened coconut, toasted (see Tip, page 22)	1/2 cup	125 mL
Ground cardamom	1/2 tsp.	2 mL
Hard margarine (or butter), melted	2 tbsp.	30 mL
Finely chopped pistachios	1 tbsp.	15 mL

Combine first 5 ingredients in large saucepan. Stir. Bring to a boil on medium. Boil gently, uncovered, for about 5 minutes, stirring often, until starting to thicken.

Add margarine. Stir until well combined. Cook for 10 to 12 minutes, stirring constantly, until mixture pulls away from side of saucepan and forms firm ball. Remove from heat. Line 9 × 5 × 3 inch (22 × 12.5 × 7.5 cm) loaf pan with foil, leaving 1 inch (2.5 cm) overhang on 2 sides. Grease foil with cooking spray. Press almond mixture evenly in pan.

Sprinkle pistachios over top. Press down lightly. Cool. Holding foil, remove fudge from pan. Discard foil. Cuts into 24 pieces.

1 piece: 89 Calories; 4.8 g Total Fat (2.2 g Mono, 0.5 g Poly, 1.9 g Sat);
   2 mg Cholesterol; 11 g Carbohydrate; trace Fibre; 1 g Protein; 20 mg Sodium

Pictured on page 131.

Photo legend, next page
Top Left: Friesens' Fudge, page 128
Top Right: Almond Pistachio Fudge, above
Bottom Right: Cherry Macadamia Fudge, this page
Bottom Left: White Chocolate Almond Fudge, page 128

Salty Sweet Peanut Chews

*A fabulous combination of sweet and salty ingredients,
these won't last long. A perfectly peanutty gift!*

Hard margarine (or butter), softened	1/2 cup	125 mL
Smooth peanut butter	1/2 cup	125 mL
Brown sugar, packed	1 cup	250 mL
Large egg	1	1
All-purpose flour	1 cup	250 mL
Baking powder	1/2 tsp.	2 mL
Baking soda	1/4 tsp.	1 mL
Salt	1/16 tsp.	0.5 mL
Miniature marshmallows	3 cups	750 mL
Peanut butter chips	1 cup	250 mL
Golden corn syrup	2/3 cup	150 mL
Hard margarine (or butter)	1/4 cup	60 mL
Vanilla	2 tsp.	10 mL
Crisp rice cereal	2 cups	500 mL
Coarsely chopped salted peanuts	2 cups	500 mL

Cream first amount of margarine, peanut butter and brown sugar in large bowl. Add egg. Beat well.

Combine next 4 ingredients in small bowl. Add to peanut butter mixture. Mix until no dry flour remains. Line 9 x 13 inch (22 x 33 cm) pan with foil, leaving 1 inch (2.5 cm) overhang on 2 sides. Grease foil with cooking spray. Spread mixture evenly in pan. Bake in 350°F (175°C) oven for about 15 minutes until edges are golden.

Immediately sprinkle with marshmallows. Bake for about 2 minutes until marshmallows start to puff. Let stand in pan on wire rack for 10 minutes.

Heat and stir next 4 ingredients in large saucepan on medium for 3 to 4 minutes until smooth.

Add cereal and peanuts. Stir well. Immediately spread evenly over marshmallows. Chill for about 1 hour until firm. Holding foil, remove mixture from pan. Discard foil. Cuts into 40 squares.

1 square: 186 Calories; 10.4 g Total Fat (5.3 g Mono, 2 g Poly, 2.4 g Sat);
6 mg Cholesterol; 22 g Carbohydrate; 1 g Fibre; 4 g Protein; 168 mg Sodium

Pictured on page 133.

Chewy Energy Bars

*Know a fitness fanatic? They'll love receiving
a Christmas tin filled with these healthy, delicious treats!*

Quick-cooking rolled oats (not instant)	2 cups	500 mL
Dark raisins	1/2 cup	125 mL
Dried cranberries	1/2 cup	125 mL
Chopped dried apricot	1/2 cup	125 mL
Unsalted roasted sunflower seeds	1/2 cup	125 mL
Pine nuts	1/2 cup	125 mL
Chopped pecans	1/2 cup	125 mL
Golden corn syrup	3/4 cup	175 mL
Hard margarine (or butter)	2 tbsp.	30 mL
Smooth peanut butter	2 tbsp.	30 mL
Shelled pumpkin seeds (or unsalted peanuts), crushed (optional)	1/4 cup	60 mL

Combine first 7 ingredients in large bowl.

Heat and stir corn syrup, margarine and peanut butter in small saucepan on medium for 3 to 5 minutes until margarine is melted and mixture is hot but not boiling. Add to rolled oats mixture. Mix well. Line 8 x 8 inch (20 x 20 cm) pan with foil, leaving 1 inch (2.5 cm) overhang on 2 sides. Grease foil with cooking spray. Press mixture evenly in pan. Cover. Chill for about 1 hour until firm. Holding foil, remove mixture from pan. Discard foil. Cut mixture in half. Cut each half crosswise into 5 bars.

Press bottom of each bar in pumpkin seeds in small shallow dish until coated. Wrap bars individually in plastic wrap. Store at room temperature for up to 2 weeks or freeze for up to 3 months. Makes 10 bars.

1 bar: 372 Calories; 17.8 g Total Fat (7.7 g Mono, 6.6 g Poly, 2.5 g Sat);
0 mg Cholesterol; 51 g Carbohydrate; 7 g Fibre; 9 g Protein; 77 mg Sodium

Pictured on page 133.

Top: Tea Time Cookie Bars, page 134
Centre: Salty Sweet Peanut Chews, this page
Bottom: Chewy Energy Bars, above

Tea Time Cookie Bars

Any time's a good time for a treat, but tea time tops the list. Chewy and sweet, with just a hint of lemon, these are perfect in a Tea Break gift basket, page 179.

Coarsely chopped whole almonds	1/4 cup	60 mL
Pecan pieces	1/4 cup	60 mL
Coarsely chopped hazelnuts (filberts)	1/4 cup	60 mL
Coarsely chopped raw cashews	1/4 cup	60 mL
Flake coconut	1/4 cup	60 mL
Dried cranberries	1/3 cup	75 mL
Golden raisins	1/3 cup	75 mL
White chocolate chips	1/3 cup	75 mL
Grated lemon zest	2 tsp.	10 mL
Tube of refrigerator sugar cookie dough	13 oz.	368 g

Spread first 5 ingredients evenly in ungreased shallow pan. Bake in 350°F (175°C) oven for 5 to 10 minutes, stirring or shaking often, until toasted. Transfer to large bowl. Cool.

Add next 4 ingredients. Stir.

Break sugar cookie dough into small pieces. Add to nut mixture. Mix well. Press evenly in greased 9 x 9 inch (22 x 22 cm) pan. Bake in 350°F (175°C) oven for about 25 minutes until wooden pick inserted in centre comes out clean. Cool. Cuts into 30 bars.

1 bar: 104 Calories; 6.2 g Total Fat (3.3 g Mono, 0.8 g Poly, 1.7 g Sat);
    4 mg Cholesterol; 12 g Carbohydrate; 1 g Fibre; 1 g Protein; 54 mg Sodium

Pictured on page 133 and on pages 178/179.

Tiny Tims

So sweet, so rich, so tempting. These treats are cut bite-size for easy eating. Package some in a decorative box and give to a friend!

Pastry for 2 crust, 9 inch (22 cm) pie, your own or a mix	1	1
Milk chocolate bars (3 1/2 oz., 100 g, each), coarsely chopped	2	2
Brown sugar, packed	2 cups	500 mL
Large eggs	3	3
All-purpose flour	1/3 cup	75 mL
Hard margarine (or butter), softened	1/3 cup	75 mL
Vanilla	2 tsp.	10 mL
Salt	1/4 tsp.	1 mL

Roll out pastry on lightly floured surface to 9 x 13 inch (22 x 33 cm) rectangle. Line bottom of greased 9 x 13 inch (22 x 33 cm) pan with pastry.

Scatter chocolate evenly over pastry.

Beat remaining 6 ingredients in large bowl until well combined. Spread evenly over chocolate. Bake in 400°F (205°C) oven for 25 to 30 minutes until wooden pick inserted in centre comes out clean. Cool. Cuts into 88 squares.

1 square: 57 Calories; 2.5 g Total Fat (1.2 g Mono, 0.2 g Poly, 0.9 g Sat);
    8 mg Cholesterol; 8 g Carbohydrate; trace Fibre; 1 g Protein; 40 mg Sodium

Pictured below.

Tiny Tims, above

Left: Bliss Bars, page 136

Right: Fruit And Honey Bars, below

Fruit And Honey Bars

*Rich, dense and filled with fruit and honey,
these bars are the perfect holiday treat.
Great as a gift for a teacher or co-worker.*

Coarsely chopped pitted dates	1 cup	250 mL
Golden raisins	1 cup	250 mL
Chopped dried figs	1 cup	250 mL
Chopped glazed pineapple	1 cup	250 mL
Halved red glazed cherries	1 cup	250 mL
Coarsely chopped walnuts	1 cup	250 mL
Large eggs	3	3
Liquid honey	1/2 cup	125 mL
All-purpose flour	1 1/2 cups	375 mL

Combine first 6 ingredients in large bowl.

Beat eggs and honey in small bowl until well combined. Add to fruit mixture. Stir well.

Add flour. Mix well. Spray 9 x 13 inch (22 x 33 cm) pan with cooking spray. Line pan with parchment (not waxed) paper, leaving 1 inch (2.5 cm) overhang on both long sides. Spread fruit mixture evenly in pan. Bake in 325°F (160°C) oven for about 45 minutes until wooden pick inserted in centre comes out clean. Cool. Holding parchment paper, remove fruit mixture from pan. Discard parchment paper. Cuts into 64 bars.

1 bar: 81 Calories; 1.5 g Total Fat (0.4 g Mono, 0.8 g Poly, 0.2 g Sat); 10 mg Cholesterol; 17 g Carbohydrate; 1 g Fibre; 1 g Protein; 4 mg Sodium

Pictured above.

Bliss Bars

A chocolate chip cookie base topped with chewy golden goodness—true bliss! Wrap some in a festive gift box and give with a package of assorted herbal teas.

Hard margarine (or butter), softened	3/4 cup	175 mL
Brown sugar, packed	3/4 cup	175 mL
Large egg	1	1
Vanilla	1 tsp.	5 mL
All-purpose flour	1 1/3 cups	325 mL
Baking powder	1/2 tsp.	2 mL
Salt	1/4 tsp.	1 mL
Semi-sweet chocolate chips	1 cup	250 mL
Chocolate wafer crumbs	1/2 cup	125 mL
Butterscotch chips	1 cup	250 mL
Flake coconut	1 1/4 cups	300 mL
Finely chopped pecans	1/3 cup	75 mL
Can of sweetened condensed milk	11 oz.	300 mL

Cream margarine and brown sugar in large bowl. Add egg. Beat well. Add vanilla. Beat until smooth.

Combine flour, baking powder and salt in small bowl. Add to margarine mixture. Mix until no dry flour remains.

Add chocolate chips. Mix well. Spread evenly in greased 9 x 13 inch (22 x 33 cm) pan.

Sprinkle next 4 ingredients, in order given, over chocolate chip mixture.

Drizzle condensed milk over pecans. Bake in 350°F (175°C) oven for about 25 minutes until edges are golden and topping is set. Cool. Cuts into 36 bars.

1 bar: 185 Calories; 9.9 g Total Fat (4.2 g Mono, 0.8 g Poly, 4.4 g Sat); 10 mg Cholesterol; 24 g Carbohydrate; 1 g Fibre; 2 g Protein; 99 mg Sodium

Pictured on page 135.

Coco-Nut Brownies

Moist, fudgey and coco-nutty. A simply scrumptious treat to give away!

Hard margarine (or butter)	1/2 cup	125 mL
Granulated sugar	1 cup	250 mL
Cocoa, sifted if lumpy	1/3 cup	75 mL
Large eggs	2	2
Vanilla	1 tsp.	5 mL
All-purpose flour	1 cup	250 mL
Salt	1/4 tsp.	1 mL
Hard margarine (or butter)	2 tbsp.	30 mL
Brown sugar, packed	1/4 cup	60 mL
Salt	1/8 tsp.	0.5 mL
Flake coconut	3/4 cup	175 mL
Chopped walnuts	1/2 cup	125 mL
Chopped pecans	1/4 cup	60 mL

Melt first amount of margarine in medium saucepan on medium. Add granulated sugar and cocoa. Heat and stir for about 3 minutes until sugar is just dissolved. Remove from heat.

Add eggs 1 at a time, beating well after each addition. Add vanilla. Beat until smooth.

Combine flour and salt in small bowl. Add to chocolate mixture. Mix until no dry flour remains. Spread evenly in greased 8 x 8 inch (22 x 22 cm) pan.

Melt second amount of margarine in small saucepan on medium. Remove from heat.

Add remaining 5 ingredients, in order given, stirring after each addition until well combined. Spoon evenly onto batter. Press down lightly. Bake in 350°F (175°C) oven for 25 to 30 minutes until top is golden and wooden pick inserted in centre comes out clean. Cool. Cut into 16 squares. Cut each square in half diagonally. Makes 32 brownies.

1 brownie: 122 Calories; 7.5 g Total Fat (3.3 g Mono, 1.4 g Poly, 2.4 g Sat); 13 mg Cholesterol; 13 g Carbohydrate; 1 g Fibre; 2 g Protein; 78 mg Sodium

Pictured on page 137.

Chocolate Cashew Brownies

These double chocolate treats make a delightful gift. Moist and rich—just like a brownie should be. An irresistible gift!

Can of sweetened condensed milk	11 oz.	300 mL
Hard margarine (or butter)	1/2 cup	125 mL
Cocoa, sifted if lumpy	1/2 cup	125 mL
Milk	1/2 cup	125 mL
Brown sugar, packed	3/4 cup	175 mL
All-purpose flour	2/3 cup	150 mL
Salt	1/8 tsp.	0.5 mL
Large eggs, fork-beaten	2	2
Semi-sweet chocolate baking squares (1 oz., 28 g, each), chopped	7	7
Coarsely chopped raw cashews, toasted (see Tip, page 22)	1/2 cup	125 mL

Heat and stir first 4 ingredients in medium saucepan on medium-low for about 5 minutes until margarine is melted. Remove from heat.

Combine brown sugar, flour and salt in small bowl. Add to milk mixture. Add egg. Stir until smooth. Cool.

Add chocolate and cashews. Mix well. Line 9 x 9 inch (22 x 22 cm) pan with foil, leaving 1 inch (2.5 cm) overhang on 2 sides. Grease foil with cooking spray. Spread mixture evenly in pan. Bake in 350°F (175°C) oven for about 35 minutes until just firm and wooden pick inserted in centre comes out moist but not wet with batter. Do not overbake. Cool. Cover. Chill for at least 6 hours or overnight. Holding foil, remove brownies from pan. Discard foil. Cuts into 36 squares.

1 square: 132 Calories; 6.7 g Total Fat (3.3 g Mono, 0.6 g Poly, 2.5 g Sat); 16 mg Cholesterol; 17 g Carbohydrate; 1 g Fibre; 2 g Protein; 62 mg Sodium

Pictured below.

Top: Coco-Nut Brownies, page 136

Bottom: Chocolate Cashew Brownies, above

Pink Chocolate Truffles

Absolutely divine! A raspberry centre hides in white chocolate bonbons accented with pretty pink decoration. An elegant part of a Stress Buster gift basket, page 178.

White chocolate chips	1 cup	250 mL
Whipping cream	2 tbsp.	30 mL
Butter (not margarine)	1 tbsp.	15 mL
Drops of red liquid food colouring	1 – 2	1 – 2
Raspberry jam	3 tbsp.	50 mL
Raspberry-flavoured liqueur (such as Chambord)	2 tbsp.	30 mL
White chocolate melting wafers	1 cup	250 mL
Pink candy melting wafers	1/4 cup	60 mL

Heat white chocolate chips, whipping cream and butter in heavy medium saucepan on lowest heat, stirring often, until chips are almost melted. Do not overheat. Remove from heat. Stir until smooth.

Add food colouring 1 drop at a time, stirring after each addition until mixture is light pink.

Press jam through sieve into medium bowl. Discard seeds. Add liqueur. Stir. Add white chocolate mixture. Stir well. Cover. Chill for about 2 hours, stirring occasionally, until firm enough to roll into balls. Roll into balls, using 2 tsp. (10 mL) for each. Place on waxed paper-lined baking sheet. Freeze for about 1 hour until firm.

Heat white chocolate wafers in small heavy saucepan on lowest heat, stirring often, until almost melted. Do not overheat. Remove from heat. Stir until smooth. Place 1 ball on top of fork. Dip into chocolate until completely coated, allowing excess to drip back into pan. Place on same waxed paper-lined baking sheet. Repeat with remaining balls and chocolate. Let stand for about 1 hour until set. May be chilled to speed setting.

Heat pink candy wafers in separate small heavy saucepan on lowest heat, stirring often, until almost melted. Do not overheat. Remove from heat. Stir until smooth. Spoon into piping bag fitted with small writing tip or into small resealable freezer bag with tiny piece snipped off corner. Drizzle pink candy in decorative pattern onto each ball. Let stand until set. Makes about 20 truffles.

1 truffle: 131 Calories; 7.2 g Total Fat (2.3 g Mono, 0.2 g Poly, 4.3 g Sat); 8 mg Cholesterol; 15 g Carbohydrate; trace Fibre; 1 g Protein; 26 mg Sodium

Pictured on front cover and on page 178.

Hazelnut Truffles

Rich, bittersweet chocolate candy enveloping crunchy hazelnuts is a not-too-sweet gift for someone who's already sweet enough!

Brown sugar, packed	1/3 cup	75 mL
Hard margarine (or butter)	3 tbsp.	50 mL
Golden corn syrup	3 tbsp.	50 mL
Cocoa, sifted if lumpy	2 tbsp.	30 mL
Vanilla	1/2 tsp.	2 mL
Finely chopped flaked hazelnuts (filberts), toasted (see Tip, page 22)	1 cup	250 mL
Whole hazelnuts (filberts), skins removed (see Tip, page 34) and toasted (see Tip, page 22)	16	16
Finely chopped flaked hazelnuts (filberts), toasted (see Tip, page 22)	1/4 cup	60 mL

Heat and stir first 5 ingredients in heavy medium saucepan on medium for about 2 minutes until margarine is melted and sugar is dissolved. Remove from heat.

Add first amount of chopped hazelnuts. Mix well. Roll into balls, using 1 tbsp. (15 mL) for each.

Push 1 whole hazelnut into centre of each ball. Roll balls to enclose hazelnuts in chocolate mixture.

Roll each ball in second amount of chopped hazelnuts in small shallow dish until coated. Makes about 16 truffles.

1 truffle: 117 Calories; 8.9 g Total Fat (6.6 g Mono, 0.9 g Poly, 1 g Sat); 0 mg Cholesterol; 10 g Carbohydrate; 1 g Fibre; 2 g Protein; 33 mg Sodium

Pictured on front cover and on page 139.

Top Left: Chocolate Mint Bark, page 140
Centre Right: Chocolate Fruit And Nut Balls, page 140
Bottom Left: Hazelnut Truffles, above

Chocolate Fruit And Nut Balls

*Set these in candy cups and include in a box
of mixed sweets along with Hazelnut Truffles and
Pink Chocolate Truffles, page 138. A decadent gift.*

White chocolate baking squares (1 oz., 28 g, each), chopped	12	12
Chopped pecans, toasted (see Tip, page 22)	1 cup	250 mL
Chopped pitted dates	2/3 cup	150 mL
Chopped glazed pineapple	1/2 cup	125 mL
Medium unsweetened coconut, toasted (see Tip, page 22)	1 1/4 cups	300 mL

Heat white chocolate in heavy medium saucepan on lowest heat, stirring often, until almost melted. Do not overheat. Remove from heat. Stir until smooth.

Add pecans, dates and pineapple. Mix well. Roll into balls, using 2 tsp. (10 mL) for each.

Roll 1 ball in coconut in small shallow dish until coated. Place on waxed paper-lined baking sheet. Repeat with remaining balls and coconut. Chill for about 30 minutes until firm. Store at room temperature in airtight container for up to 2 months. Makes about 38 balls.

1 ball: 107 Calories; 6.9 g Total Fat (2.3 g Mono, 0.6 g Poly, 3.5 g Sat); 2 mg Cholesterol; 11 g Carbohydrate; 1 g Fibre; 1 g Protein; 9 mg Sodium

Pictured on page 139.

Mocha Truffles

Candy cup ruffles will show off these truffles—a beautiful chocolate display! Wrap in a cellophane Gift Wrap Cone, page 142, to give to a friend or neighbour.

Whipping cream	1/3 cup	75 mL
Hard margarine (or butter)	1 tbsp.	15 mL
Instant coffee granules	1 tsp.	5 mL
Semi-sweet chocolate baking squares (1 oz., 28 g, each), chopped	10	10
White chocolate melting wafers	1 1/3 cups	325 mL
Cocoa, sifted if lumpy	2 tsp.	10 mL

Heat and stir whipping cream, margarine and coffee granules in heavy medium saucepan on medium for 3 to 4 minutes until coffee granules are dissolved.

Add semi-sweet chocolate. Heat on lowest heat, stirring often, until chocolate is almost melted. Do not overheat. Remove from heat. Stir until smooth. Transfer to medium bowl. Cover. Chill for about 2 hours until firm enough to roll into balls. Roll into 3/4 inch (2 cm) balls. Place on waxed paper-lined baking sheet. Chill for about 1 hour until firm.

Heat white chocolate in small heavy saucepan on lowest heat, stirring often, until almost melted. Do not overheat. Remove from heat. Stir until smooth. Place 1 ball on top of fork. Dip into chocolate until completely coated, allowing excess to drip back into pan. Place on same waxed paper-lined baking sheet. Repeat with remaining balls and chocolate.

Dust balls with cocoa before chocolate sets. Chill for 1 hour. Makes about 30 truffles.

1 truffle: 99 Calories; 6.5 g Total Fat (2.2 g Mono, 0.2 g Poly, 3.7 g Sat); 5 mg Cholesterol; 11 g Carbohydrate; 1 g Fibre; 1 g Protein; 14 mg Sodium

Pictured on page 6 and on page 141.

Chocolate Mint Bark

This double chocolate treat makes an enticing stocking stuffer or a perfect part of a Chocolate Lover's gift basket, page 172.

Dark chocolate bars (3 1/2 oz., 100 g, each), chopped	5	5
Package of mint cream-filled chocolate cookies, chopped	12 oz.	325 g

Heat chocolate in large heavy saucepan on lowest heat, stirring often, until almost melted. Do not overheat. Remove from heat. Stir until smooth.

Add cookies. Mix well. Spread evenly in waxed paper-lined baking sheet with sides. Chill for about 1 hour until set. Remove from pan. Break bark into irregular-shaped pieces, about 1 1/2 x 4 inches (3.8 x 10 cm) each. Makes about 24 pieces.

1 piece: 164 Calories; 9 g Total Fat (3.7 g Mono, 0.6 g Poly, 4.3 g Sat); 0 mg Cholesterol; 23 g Carbohydrate; 2 g Fibre; 2 g Protein; 84 mg Sodium

Pictured on page 139 and on page 175.

Light Coloured: Mocha Truffles, this page, in Gift Wrap Cone, page 142
Dark Coloured: Pecan Truffles in Gift Wrap Cone, page 142

Pecan Truffles

These delicious sweets boast creamy, coffee-flavoured centres. Mix them with Mocha Truffles, page 140, and place into a Gift Wrap Cone, this page. Tuck them into a Good Neighbour gift basket, page 184.

Whipping cream	1/2 cup	125 mL
Milk chocolate bars (3 1/2 oz., 100 g, each), chopped	2	2
Finely chopped pecans, toasted (see Tip, page 22)	1/2 cup	125 mL
Coffee-flavoured liqueur (such as Kahlúa)	1 tbsp.	15 mL
Semi-sweet chocolate baking squares (1 oz., 28 g, each), chopped	8	8
White chocolate baking squares (1 oz., 28 g, each), chopped	2	2

Heat whipping cream in heavy medium saucepan on medium until hot and bubbles form around edge of saucepan. Remove from heat.

Add milk chocolate. Stir until smooth.

Add pecans and liqueur. Stir well. Transfer to small bowl. Cover. Chill for about 2 1/2 hours until firm enough to roll into balls. Roll into balls, using 2 tsp. (10 mL) for each. Place on waxed paper-lined baking sheet. Chill for about 30 minutes until firm.

Heat semi-sweet chocolate in small heavy saucepan on lowest heat, stirring often, until almost melted. Do not overheat. Remove from heat. Stir until smooth. Place 1 ball on top of fork. Dip into chocolate until completely coated, allowing excess to drip back into pan. Place on same waxed paper-lined baking sheet. Repeat with remaining balls and chocolate. Chill for about 1 hour until set.

Heat white chocolate in separate small heavy saucepan on lowest heat, stirring often, until almost melted. Do not overheat. Remove from heat. Stir until smooth. Spoon into small piping bag fitted with small writing tip or into small resealable freezer bag with tiny piece snipped off corner. Drizzle white chocolate in decorative pattern over each ball. Chill until set. Makes about 36 truffles.

1 truffle: 90 Calories; 6.3 g Total Fat (2.4 g Mono, 0.5 g Poly, 3.2 g Sat); 6 mg Cholesterol; 9 g Carbohydrate; 1 g Fibre; 1 g Protein; 8 mg Sodium

Pictured on page 6, on page 141 and on page 184.

★ Gift Wrap Cone ★

A pretty way to present a gift of truffles or fudge. Great as a party favour, too. Be sure to use a heavier paper for best results.

MATERIALS
Decorative paper (12 x 12 inches, 30 x 30 cm)
Decorative beads or other embellishments
Garland
Cellophane (12 x 12 inches, 30 x 30 cm)

TOOLS
dinner plate, pencil, scissors, ruler, glue gun

Using a dinner plate, trace a circle onto the wrong side of the paper and cut it out. Draw 2 lines across the diameter of the circle to intersect at the centre. Measure and mark 1 1/2 inches (3.8 cm) from the end of 1 line along the edge of the circle. Draw a line from the mark to the centre of the circle. Cut out and discard the resulting pie-shaped piece.

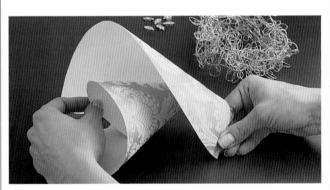

Slide 1 edge of the cut-out over the other until they meet to make a cone (see picture). Glue in place. Glue 1 end of the garland to the pointed end of the cone and loosely wrap around the cone toward the open end. Glue the other end of the garland to the inside of the open end of the cone. Decorate the cone with beads or other embellishments as desired.

Make a cone the same size using cellophane. Use it to line the paper cone.

Pictured on page 6 and on page 141.

Chocolate Cranberry Rum Balls

These say Merry Christmas through and through—a special treat made just for you!

Dried cranberries	1 cup	250 mL
Dark (navy) rum	1/3 cup	75 mL
Finely crushed vanilla wafers (about 70 wafers)	2 1/2 cups	625 mL
Ground pecans, toasted (see Tip, page 22)	1 1/2 cups	375 mL
Icing (confectioner's) sugar	1/3 cup	75 mL
Hard margarine (or butter), melted	1/3 cup	75 mL
White chocolate baking squares (1 oz., 28 g, each), chopped	14	14
Chocolate sprinkles (optional)		

Measure cranberries into small bowl. Add rum. Stir well. Let stand for 1 hour.

Combine next 4 ingredients in large bowl. Add cranberry mixture. Mix well. Shape into balls, using 1 tbsp. (15 mL) for each. Place on waxed paper-lined baking sheet. Let stand for about 1 hour until firm.

Heat white chocolate in small heavy saucepan on lowest heat, stirring often, until almost melted. Do not overheat. Remove from heat. Stir until smooth. Place 1 ball on top of fork. Dip into chocolate until completely coated, allowing excess to drip back into pan. Place on same waxed paper-lined baking sheet. Repeat with remaining balls and chocolate.

Sprinkle balls with chocolate sprinkles before white chocolate sets. Chill for 1 hour. Makes about 50 rum balls.

1 rum ball: 108 Calories; 6.8 g Total Fat (3.4 g Mono, 1 g Poly, 2 g Sat); 4 mg Cholesterol; 10 g Carbohydrate; 1 g Fibre; 1 g Protein; 35 mg Sodium

Pictured below.

Almond Fruit Bark

A tempting fruit-and-nut chocolate treat. Package in decorative Christmas tins for gift giving.

Dark (or white) chocolate bars (3 1/2 oz.,100 g, each), chopped	4	4
Dried cherries	1/2 cup	125 mL
Whole natural almonds, toasted (see Tip, page 22)	1/2 cup	125 mL
Chopped dried apricot	1/3 cup	75 mL

Heat chocolate in heavy medium saucepan on lowest heat, stirring often, until almost melted. Do not overheat. Remove from heat. Stir until smooth.

Add cherries, almonds and apricot. Mix well. Spread evenly in waxed paper-lined baking sheet with sides. Chill for about 30 minutes until set. Remove from pan. Break bark into irregular-shaped pieces, about 1 1/2 x 4 inches (3.8 x 10 cm) each. Freeze for up to 1 month. Makes about 24 pieces.

1 piece: 112 Calories; 6.8 g Total Fat (2.8 g Mono, 0.5 g Poly, 3.1 g Sat); 0 mg Cholesterol; 14 g Carbohydrate; 1 g Fibre; 2 g Protein; 2 mg Sodium

Pictured on page 145.

Dalmatian Bark

A gift that's all bark and no bite! Wrap this spotted candy with a stuffed toy Dalmatian puppy for a gift kids will love.

White chocolate bars (3 1/2 oz., 100 g, each), chopped	5	5
Semi-sweet chocolate chips	1/2 cup	125 mL

Line 9 x 13 inch (22 x 33 cm) pan with waxed paper, leaving 1 inch (2.5 cm) overhang on both long sides. Set aside. Heat white chocolate in heavy medium saucepan on lowest heat, stirring often, until almost melted. Do not overheat. Remove from heat. Stir until smooth. Spread evenly in pan.

Sprinkle with chocolate chips, creating an uneven pattern like a Dalmatian's spots. Gently tap pan on work surface to settle chips into chocolate. Chill for about 2 hours until set. Holding waxed paper, remove bark from pan. Discard waxed paper. Break bark into irregular-shaped pieces, about 1 1/2 x 4 inches (3.8 x 10 cm) each. Makes about 18 pieces.

1 piece: 172 Calories; 9.9 g Total Fat (3.2 g Mono, 0.3 g Poly, 5.8 g Sat); 6 mg Cholesterol; 20 g Carbohydrate; trace Fibre; 2 g Protein; 25 mg Sodium

Pictured on page 145.

Ginger Chocolate Cups

Bold ginger flavour accents creamy milk chocolate. A snap to make and easy to give away! Wrap a few in cellophane as party favours, or put a dozen into a festive gift box for a more substantial gift.

Milk chocolate bars (3 1/2 oz., 100 g, each), coarsely chopped	4	4
Coarsely chopped crystallized ginger	1 cup	250 mL
Foil (or paper) candy cups (1 1/4 inch, 3 cm, diameter)	30	30
Minced crystallized ginger	1 tbsp.	15 mL

Heat chocolate in heavy medium saucepan on lowest heat, stirring often, until almost melted. Do not overheat. Remove from heat. Stir until smooth.

Add first amount of ginger. Mix well. Spoon into candy cups set in miniature muffin cups.

Sprinkle with second amount of ginger. Chill for about 30 minutes until set. Makes 30 cups.

1 cup: 78 Calories; 4.1 g Total Fat (1.3 g Mono, 0.1 g Poly, 2.5 g Sat); 3 mg Cholesterol; 10 g Carbohydrate; trace Fibre; 1 g Protein; 13 mg Sodium

Pictured on page 118 and on page 145.

Top Left: Dalmatian Bark, this page
Top Right: Almond Fruit Bark, this page
Bottom: Ginger Chocolate Cups, above

Twist on Tradition

Christmas is a time of year to honour family traditions, both old and new, and it's these annual customs that make each family gathering memorable. This wonderful collection of recipes reflects many of the season's flavourful traditions, delivered with a refreshingly clever "twist," such as smooth chocolate eggnog pudding or spicy gingerbread pull-aparts.

Before the holiday rush demands too much of your time, think about making a rich, indulgent fruitcake. This lovely culinary tradition can be created early in the season because the fruitcakes actually need time to sit while the flavours ripen. And you can get a jump-start on baking your breads, cookies and squares as well. Simply freeze them in advance and add colourful decorations or icing just before delivering them to family and friends.

Braided Fruit Bread

Three beautiful loaves, gently spiced and speckled with fruit.
Wrap a loaf in a pretty Christmas tea towel as
a warm hostess gift for a holiday brunch.

Dark raisins	1/2 cup	125 mL
Golden raisins	1/2 cup	125 mL
Chopped pitted dates	1/2 cup	125 mL
Chopped red glazed cherries	1/2 cup	125 mL
Almond-flavoured liqueur (such as Amaretto)	1/3 cup	75 mL
Diced mixed peel	1/4 cup	60 mL
Slivered almonds, toasted (See Tip, page 22)	1/2 cup	125 mL
Warm water	1 1/2 cups	375 mL
Granulated sugar	2 tsp.	10 mL
Envelopes of active dry yeast (1/4 oz., 8 g, each), or 2 tbsp. (30 mL) plus 3/4 tsp. (4 mL)	3	3
All-purpose flour	5 cups	1.25 L
Granulated sugar	3 tbsp.	50 mL
Ground cinnamon	2 tsp.	10 mL
Salt	1 tsp.	5 mL
Ground nutmeg	1/2 tsp.	2 mL
Large eggs, fork-beaten	2	2
Hard margarine (or butter), melted	1/4 cup	60 mL
All-purpose flour, approximately	2/3 cup	150 mL
Large egg, fork-beaten	1	1
ALMOND GLAZE		
Icing (confectioner's) sugar	1 cup	250 mL
Milk	1 1/2 tbsp.	25 mL
Hard margarine (or butter), softened	2 tsp.	10 mL
Almond flavouring	1/4 tsp.	1 mL

Combine first 6 ingredients in medium bowl. Cover. Let stand for at least 6 hours or overnight, stirring occasionally.

Add almonds. Stir. Set aside.

Stir warm water and first amount of sugar in small bowl until sugar is dissolved. Sprinkle yeast over top. Let stand for 10 minutes. Stir until yeast is dissolved.

Combine next 5 ingredients in extra-large bowl. Make a well in centre.

Add yeast and fruit mixtures, first amount of egg and margarine to well. Mix until soft dough forms.

Turn out dough onto lightly floured surface. Knead for 5 to 10 minutes, adding second amount of flour 1 tbsp. (15 mL) at a time if necessary to prevent sticking, until smooth and elastic. Place in greased extra-large bowl, turning once to grease top. Cover with greased waxed paper and tea towel. Let stand in oven with light on and door closed for about 1 3/4 hours until doubled in bulk.

Punch dough down. Turn out onto lightly floured surface. Knead for about 1 minute until smooth. Divide dough into 3 equal portions. Divide 1 portion into 3 equal pieces. Keep remaining 2 portions covered to prevent drying. Roll each piece into 12 inch (30 cm) long rope with slightly tapered ends. Lay ropes side by side along length of work surface. Pinch ropes together at one end. Braid. Pinch together at opposite end. Tuck ends under. Place on greased baking sheet. Cover with tea towel. Repeat with remaining 2 portions, placing braids about 2 inches (5 cm) apart on separate greased baking sheet.

Brush each braid evenly with second amount of egg. Let stand in oven with light on and door closed for about 30 minutes until almost doubled in size. Bake in 350°F (175°C) oven for 25 to 30 minutes, switching position of baking sheets at halftime, until golden brown and hollow sounding when tapped. Immediately transfer loaves to wire racks to cool.

Almond Glaze: Beat all 4 ingredients in small bowl, adding more icing sugar or milk if necessary, until barely pourable consistency. Makes about 6 tbsp. (100 mL) glaze. Drizzle about 2 tbsp. (30 mL) over each braid. Let stand until set. Each loaf cuts into 12 slices, for a total of 36 slices.

1 slice: 171 Calories; 3.3 g Total Fat (1.9 g Mono, 0.5 g Poly, 0.6 g Sat);
18 mg Cholesterol; 31 g Carbohydrate; 1 g Fibre; 4 g Protein; 92 mg Sodium

Pictured on page 149.

Photo legend, next page
Left: Gingerbread Pull-Aparts, page 150
Right: Braided Fruit Bread, this page

Gingerbread Pull-Aparts

*Give these tender, ginger-spiced rolls in a bright,
festive tin along with a jar of Two Berry Jam, page 84,
to enjoy on Christmas morning.*

Warm water	1/2 cup	125 mL
Granulated sugar	1 tsp.	5 mL
Envelope of active dry yeast (or 2 1/4 tsp., 11 mL)	1/4 oz.	8 g
Brown sugar, packed	1/4 cup	60 mL
Milk	2 tbsp.	30 mL
Fancy (mild) molasses	2 tbsp.	30 mL
Hard margarine (or butter)	1 1/2 tbsp.	25 mL
Salt	3/4 tsp.	4 mL
All-purpose flour	1 1/2 cups	375 mL
Ground ginger	1 1/2 tsp.	7 mL
Ground cinnamon	1/2 tsp.	2 mL
Ground cloves	1/4 tsp.	1 mL
Large egg, fork-beaten	1	1
All-purpose flour	1 1/4 cups	300 mL
All-purpose flour, approximately	1/4 cup	60 mL
Hard margarine (or butter), melted	1 1/2 tsp.	7 mL

Stir warm water and granulated sugar in medium bowl until
sugar is dissolved. Sprinkle yeast over top. Let stand for
10 minutes. Stir until yeast is dissolved.

Combine next 5 ingredients in small saucepan. Heat and stir
on medium for about 2 minutes until margarine is melted
and brown sugar is dissolved. Remove from heat. Let stand
for 5 minutes to cool slightly. Add to yeast mixture. Stir well.

Combine next 4 ingredients in large bowl. Make a well
in centre.

Add yeast mixture and egg to well. Stir until smooth.

Add second amount of flour 1/4 cup (60 mL) at a time,
mixing until soft dough forms.

Turn out dough onto lightly floured surface. Knead for 5 to
10 minutes, adding third amount of flour 1 tbsp. (15 mL) at a
time if necessary to prevent sticking, until smooth and elastic.
Place in greased large bowl, turning once to grease top.
Cover with greased waxed paper and tea towel. Let stand in
oven with light on and door closed for about 1 1/2 hours
until doubled in bulk. Punch dough down. Turn out onto
lightly floured surface. Knead for about 1 minute until
smooth. Divide dough into 12 equal portions. Roll each
portion into ball. Arrange in single layer in greased 9 inch
(22 cm) round pan. Cover with greased waxed paper and tea
towel. Let stand in oven with light on and door closed for
about 45 minutes until doubled in size. Bake in 375°F (190°C)
oven for about 20 minutes until golden brown and hollow
sounding when tapped. Remove from oven.

Immediately brush tops of rolls with second amount of
margarine. Let stand in pan for 5 minutes before removing to
wire rack to cool. Makes 12 pull-aparts.

1 pull-apart: 177 Calories; 2.8 g Total Fat (1.5 g Mono, 0.4 g Poly, 0.6 g Sat);
   18 mg Cholesterol; 33 g Carbohydrate; 1 g Fibre; 4 g Protein; 182 mg Sodium

Pictured on page 148.

Stollen Tea Dunkers

*With Stollen (SHTOH-luhn), the flavours of a German
Christmas are baked as biscotti instead of a loaf. Give it
away in a festive teapot, along with some flavoured teas.*

Chopped mixed glazed fruit	1 cup	250 mL
Sultana raisins	1/2 cup	125 mL
Spiced rum (see Note)	3 tbsp.	50 mL
All-purpose flour	2 1/2 cups	625 mL
Granulated sugar	1 cup	250 mL
Sliced natural almonds, toasted (see Tip, page 22)	3/4 cup	175 mL
Baking powder	1 tsp.	5 mL
Salt	1/8 tsp.	0.5 mL
Large eggs	2	2
Hard margarine (or butter), melted	1/4 cup	60 mL
Grated lemon zest	1/2 tsp.	2 mL
Icing (confectioner's) sugar, for dusting		

Combine glazed fruit and raisins in medium bowl. Add rum. Stir well. Cover. Let stand at room temperature for at least 6 hours or overnight, stirring occasionally.

Combine next 5 ingredients in large bowl. Make a well in centre.

Beat eggs, margarine and lemon zest in small bowl. Add to well. Add fruit mixture. Mix until stiff dough forms. Turn out onto lightly floured surface. Knead 6 times. Divide dough in half. Roll each half into 12 inch (30 cm) long log. Arrange about 2 inches (5 cm) apart on greased baking sheet. Flatten each log slightly. Bake in 350ºF (175ºC) oven for 25 to 30 minutes until golden. Let stand on baking sheet for about 20 minutes until cool enough to handle. Cut each log diagonally with serrated knife into 3/4 inch (2 cm) slices.

Arrange evenly spaced apart on same baking sheet. Bake in 300ºF (150ºC) oven for about 30 minutes, turning once at halftime, until dry and crisp. Let stand on baking sheet for 5 minutes before removing to wire rack to cool. Dust 1/2 of each slice, on both sides, with icing sugar. Makes about 25 dunkers.

1 dunker: 163 Calories; 4.3 g Total Fat (2.6 g Mono, 0.7 g Poly, 0.7 g Sat); 17 mg Cholesterol; 28 g Carbohydrate; 1 g Fibre; 3 g Protein; 61 mg Sodium

Pictured on page 146 and above.

Note: If preferred, omit spiced rum. Use 1/2 tsp. (2 mL) rum flavouring and 2 tbsp. (30 mL) plus 2 1/2 tsp. (12 mL) orange juice.

Golden Orange Fruitcakes

Dense, chewy and delicious. These pretty little fruitcakes wrapped in cellophane will dress up a gift basket of specialty coffees and a couple of mugs.

Chopped golden raisins	1 cup	250 mL
Diced dried pineapple	1 cup	250 mL
Diced dried apricot (or peaches)	1 cup	250 mL
Diced mixed peel	1/2 cup	125 mL
Orange juice	1/3 cup	75 mL
White corn syrup	2 tbsp.	30 mL
Hard margarine (or butter), softened	1 cup	250 mL
Granulated sugar	3/4 cup	175 mL
Large eggs	4	4
Grated orange zest	2 tbsp.	30 mL
Chopped slivered almonds, toasted (see Tip, page 22)	1/2 cup	125 mL
All-purpose flour	1 1/2 cups	375 mL
Salt	1/4 tsp.	1 mL
Whole blanched almonds	90	90
Orange-flavoured liqueur (such as Grand Marnier), or orange juice	1/3 cup	75 mL

Combine first 4 ingredients in medium bowl. Set aside.

Heat and stir orange juice and corn syrup in small saucepan on medium for about 2 minutes until boiling. Add to fruit mixture. Stir well. Cover. Let stand at room temperature overnight.

Cream margarine and sugar in large bowl. Add eggs 1 at a time, beating well after each addition. Add orange zest. Beat well.

Add fruit mixture and first amount of almonds. Mix well.

Combine flour and salt in small bowl. Add to fruit mixture. Mix until no dry flour remains. Grease 18 muffin cups (see Note) with cooking spray. Fill cups 3/4 full. Smooth top of each.

Arrange 5 whole almonds in star pattern on top of batter in each muffin cup. Bake in 300°F (150°C) oven for 40 to 45 minutes until wooden pick inserted in centre of fruitcake comes out clean. Remove from oven.

Immediately brush liqueur on each fruitcake. Cover loosely with foil. Cool. Makes 18 fruitcakes.

1 fruitcake: 357 Calories; 16.7 g Total Fat (10.4 g Mono, 2.3 g Poly, 3 g Sat); 48 mg Cholesterol; 47 g Carbohydrate; 2 g Fibre; 5 g Protein; 179 mg Sodium

Pictured on page 153.

Note: To ensure even baking when you have empty muffin cups, fill empty cups with about 1/4 inch (6 mm) water.

Fig And Pecan Cakes

Moist, tender and gently sweet. Wrap individually in cellophane and tie with raffia or ribbon.

Coarsely chopped dried figs	1 cup	250 mL
Water	1 cup	250 mL
Dark raisins	1/2 cup	125 mL
Baking soda	1 tsp.	5 mL
Hard margarine (or butter), softened	1/3 cup	75 mL
Brown sugar, packed	2/3 cup	150 mL
Large eggs	2	2
Vanilla	1 tsp.	5 mL
Grated orange zest	2 tsp.	10 mL
All-purpose flour	1 1/2 cups	375 mL
Coarsely chopped pecans, toasted (see Tip, page 22)	1 cup	250 mL
Baking powder	2 tsp.	10 mL

Grease six 1 cup (250 mL) ramekins with cooking spray. Line bottom of each with waxed paper. Place ramekins on baking sheet. Set aside. Combine first 4 ingredients in medium saucepan. Bring to a boil on high. Immediately remove from heat. Let stand for about 45 minutes until cool.

Cream margarine and brown sugar in large bowl. Add eggs 1 at a time, beating well after each addition. Add vanilla. Beat until smooth.

Add fig mixture and orange zest. Mix well.

Combine flour, pecans and baking powder in small bowl. Add to fig mixture. Mix until no dry flour remains. Spoon into ramekins. Bake in 350°F (175°C) oven for about 30 minutes until golden and firm. Let stand in ramekins for 10 minutes before inverting onto wire racks. Discard waxed paper. Cool. Each cake cuts into 4 pieces, for a total of 24 pieces.

1 piece: 152 Calories; 6.8 g Total Fat (4.1 g Mono, 1.3 g Poly, 1.0 g Sat); 18 mg Cholesterol; 22 g Carbohydrate; 2 g Fibre; 2 g Protein; 125 mg Sodium

Pictured on page 153.

Top and Centre Left: Fig And Pecan Cakes, above
Centre Right and Bottom: Golden Orange Fruitcakes, this page

Chocolate Berry Fruitcake

Don't tell them it's fruitcake and they'll never know!
Infused with brandy and drizzled with raspberry liqueur
glaze, this truffle-flavoured cake is sure to be a pleasing gift.
Package it in a decorative gift box along with
a jar of the Raspberry Glaze.

Dried cranberries	1 cup	250 mL
Chopped mixed glazed fruit	1 cup	250 mL
Chopped dried pitted prunes	1/2 cup	125 mL
Chopped pitted dates	1/2 cup	125 mL
Raspberry-flavoured liqueur (such as Chambord)	1/4 cup	60 mL
Unsweetened chocolate baking squares (1 oz., 28 g, each), chopped	4	4
Hard margarine (or butter)	1/2 cup	125 mL
Whole cranberry sauce	2/3 cup	150 mL
Frozen concentrated orange juice, thawed	1/3 cup	75 mL
Large eggs	3	3
Brown sugar, packed	1 1/2 cups	375 mL
All-purpose flour	2 1/4 cups	550 mL
Chopped pecans (or walnuts)	1 cup	250 mL
Baking powder	1 tsp.	5 mL
Baking soda	1 tsp.	5 mL
Salt	1/2 tsp.	2 mL
Cocoa, sifted if lumpy	2 tsp.	10 mL
All-purpose flour	2 tsp.	10 mL
Water	1 cup	250 mL
Granulated sugar	1/2 cup	125 mL
Brandy	1/2 cup	125 mL
Cheesecloth		
Brandy, approximately	1/2 cup	125 mL
RASPBERRY GLAZE		
Raspberry-flavoured liqueur (such as Chambord)	3 tbsp.	50 mL
Icing (confectioner's) sugar	1 cup	250 mL

Combine first 5 ingredients in large bowl. Let stand for about 1 hour, stirring occasionally, until liqueur is absorbed. Set aside.

Heat chocolate and margarine in heavy medium saucepan on lowest heat, stirring often, until chocolate is almost melted. Do not overheat. Remove from heat. Stir until smooth.

Add cranberry sauce and concentrated orange juice. Stir well. Cool.

Beat eggs in separate large bowl until frothy. Add brown sugar. Beat until thick and pale. Add chocolate mixture. Beat. Add fruit mixture. Stir well.

Combine next 5 ingredients in small bowl. Add to fruit mixture. Mix until no dry flour remains.

Spray 12 cup (3 L) bundt pan with cooking spray. Combine cocoa and second amount of flour in small cup. Sprinkle in pan. Tilt pan, gently tapping, until coated with cocoa mixture. Discard any excess. Spread batter evenly in pan. Bake in 325°F (160°C) oven for about 1 1/4 hours until wooden pick inserted in centre of cake comes out clean. Let stand for 10 minutes before inverting onto wire rack set in baking sheet with sides to cool.

Heat and stir water and granulated sugar in small saucepan on high for about 2 minutes until sugar is dissolved. Remove from heat.

Add first amount of brandy. Stir well. Randomly poke several holes with skewer in top of cake. Drizzle brandy mixture over cake.

Place 4 layers of cheesecloth in medium bowl. Pour second amount of brandy over top. Let stand until brandy is absorbed, adding more brandy if necessary to soak cheesecloth. Wrap cake with cheesecloth. Wrap with waxed paper. Wrap tightly with foil. Store in refrigerator for 2 weeks. Check cake after 1 week. Moisten cheesecloth with additional brandy if necessary. Unwrap fruitcake. Place on cake plate.

Raspberry Glaze: Stir liqueur into icing sugar in small bowl, adding more liqueur or icing sugar if necessary, until barely pourable consistency. Makes about 1/2 cup (125 mL) glaze. Drizzle over fruitcake. Cuts into 16 slices.

1 slice: 553 Calories; 16.5 g Total Fat (8.9 g Mono, 2.2 g Poly, 4.3 g Sat); 40 mg Cholesterol; 86 g Carbohydrate; 5 g Fibre; 5 g Protein; 284 mg Sodium

Pictured on page 155.

Left: Chocolate Berry Fruitcake and Raspberry Glaze, this page
Top Right and Bottom: Chocolate Eggnog Pudding, page 156
Centre Right: Eggnog Sauce, page 156

Chocolate Eggnog Pudding

Place this delightful pudding in a gift basket with a jar of Eggnog Sauce to drizzle over each slice at serving time.

Large egg	1	1
Granulated sugar	1/3 cup	75 mL
Eggnog	1/2 cup	125 mL
Hard margarine (or butter), melted	2 tbsp.	30 mL
Brandy (or vanilla) flavouring	1/2 tsp.	2 mL
All-purpose flour	1 cup	250 mL
Cocoa, sifted if lumpy	2 tbsp.	30 mL
Baking powder	2 tsp.	10 mL
Ground cinnamon	1/4 tsp.	1 mL
Ground nutmeg	1/4 tsp.	1 mL
Salt	1/4 tsp.	1 mL
Boiling water		

EGGNOG SAUCE

White chocolate baking squares (1 oz., 28 g, each), chopped	4	4
Eggnog	1/2 cup	125 mL
Brandy (see Note)	1 tbsp.	15 mL

Beat egg and sugar in medium bowl until thick and pale. Set aside.

Combine eggnog, margarine and flavouring in small bowl. Set aside.

Combine next 6 ingredients in separate medium bowl. Add to egg mixture in 3 additions, alternating with eggnog mixture in 2 additions, beginning and ending with flour mixture, until no dry flour remains. Transfer to well-greased 4 cup (1 L) heatproof bowl or pudding pan. Bowl should be about 2/3 full. Cover with greased foil. Place on wire rack set in small roasting pan.

Pour boiling water into roasting pan until halfway up side of bowl. Bake in 350°F (175°C) oven for about 50 minutes until wooden pick inserted in centre comes out clean. Carefully remove bowl from water. Let stand for 5 minutes before inverting pudding onto wire rack to cool. Cuts into 8 wedges.

Eggnog Sauce: Heat white chocolate and eggnog in small heavy saucepan on lowest heat, stirring often, until chocolate is almost melted. Do not overheat. Remove from heat. Stir until smooth.

Add brandy. Stir well. Makes about 3/4 cup (175 mL) sauce. Cool. Pour into sterile jar with tight-fitting lid. Store in refrigerator for up to 8 weeks. Serve with pudding wedges. Serves 8.

1 serving: 257 Calories; 10.7 g Total Fat (4.3 g Mono, 0.7 g Poly, 4.9 g Sat); 50 mg Cholesterol; 36 g Carbohydrate; 1 g Fibre; 5 g Protein; 240 mg Sodium

Pictured on page 155.

Note: If preferred, omit brandy. Use 1/8 tsp. (0.5 mL) brandy flavouring.

Hawaiian Shortbread Squares

A sweet, tropical topping makes buttery shortbread even better. A little taste of sunshine in a Sun Seeker's gift basket, page 182, for a cold winter day.

All-purpose flour	1 cup	250 mL
Icing (confectioner's) sugar	1/2 cup	125 mL
Cold butter (not margarine), cut up	1/2 cup	125 mL
Medium banana, mashed	1	1
Can of crushed pineapple, drained	14 oz.	398 mL
Flake coconut	1 cup	250 mL
Slivered almonds	1/2 cup	125 mL
Sweetened condensed milk	1/2 cup	125 mL

Combine flour and icing sugar in medium bowl. Cut in butter until mixture resembles fine crumbs. Line 8 x 8 inch (20 x 20 cm) pan with foil, leaving 1 inch (2.5 cm) overhang on 2 sides. Grease foil with cooking spray. Press mixture evenly in pan.

Combine remaining 5 ingredients in same medium bowl. Spread evenly over shortbread mixture. Bake in 350°F (175°C) oven for 40 to 45 minutes until golden. Cool. Holding foil, remove shortbread from pan. Discard foil. Cuts into 36 squares.

1 square: 94 Calories; 5.9 g Total Fat (1.6 g Mono, 0.4 g Poly, 3.5 g Sat); 9 mg Cholesterol; 10 g Carbohydrate; 1 g Fibre; 1 g Protein; 35 mg Sodium

Pictured on page 159 and on page 183.

Panettone Cookies

An Italian Christmas tradition, panettone (pan-uh-TOH-nee) is a sweet treat full of raisins, citron and pine nuts, accented with licorice-flavoured anise. A classic combination in a cookie—what a great gift!

Hard margarine (or butter), softened	1/2 cup	125 mL
Brown sugar, packed	1/2 cup	125 mL
Granulated sugar	1/4 cup	60 mL
Large egg	1	1
Almond flavouring	1/4 tsp.	1 mL
All-purpose flour	1 1/4 cups	300 mL
Aniseed, crushed	1/2 tsp.	2 mL
Baking soda	1/2 tsp.	2 mL
Salt	1/4 tsp.	1 mL
Pine nuts, toasted (see Tip, page 22)	1/4 cup	60 mL
Golden raisins	2 tbsp.	30 mL
Dark raisins	2 tbsp.	30 mL
Finely chopped citron peel	1 tbsp.	15 mL

Cream margarine and both sugars in large bowl. Add egg. Beat well. Add flavouring. Beat until smooth.

Combine next 4 ingredients in small bowl. Add to margarine mixture. Mix until no dry flour remains.

Add remaining 4 ingredients. Mix well. Drop, using 2 tsp. (10 mL) for each, about 2 inches (5 cm) apart onto ungreased cookie sheets. Bake in 375°F (190°C) oven for 6 to 8 minutes until edges are golden. Let stand on cookie sheets for 5 minutes before removing to wire racks to cool. Makes 4 1/2 dozen (54) cookies.

1 cookie: 47 Calories; 2.3 g Total Fat (1.4 g Mono, 0.4 g Poly, 0.5 g Sat); 4 mg Cholesterol; 6 g Carbohydrate; trace Fibre; 1 g Protein; 47 mg Sodium

Pictured below.

Tropical Fruitcakes

Wrap these flavourful fruitcakes individually in cellophane and put in a Sun Seeker's gift basket, page 182, to warm someone's heart this season.

Hard margarine (or butter), softened	1/2 cup	125 mL
Brown sugar, packed	3/4 cup	175 mL
Large eggs	2	2
Coconut flavouring	1 tsp.	5 mL
Spiced rum	1/4 cup	60 mL
Pineapple juice	1/4 cup	60 mL
Golden corn syrup	2 tbsp.	30 mL
Finely grated, peeled gingerroot	1 tsp.	5 mL
All-purpose flour	1 1/2 cups	375 mL
Baking powder	1/2 tsp.	2 mL
Baking soda	1/4 tsp.	1 mL
Chopped dried pineapple	3/4 cup	175 mL
Chopped dried mango	1/2 cup	125 mL
Chopped dried cantaloupe	1/4 cup	60 mL
Flake coconut	1/4 cup	60 mL
Chopped raw macadamia nuts	1/4 cup	60 mL
Chopped Brazil nuts	1/4 cup	60 mL
Spiced rum	3 tbsp.	50 mL
Cheesecloth squares (9 inches, 22 cm, each)	12	12
Spiced rum, approximately	1/4 cup	60 mL
COCONUT GLAZE		
Icing (confectioner's) sugar	1/4 cup	60 mL
Pineapple juice	2 tsp.	10 mL
Coconut flavouring	1/8 tsp.	0.5 mL

Cream margarine and brown sugar in large bowl. Add eggs 1 at a time, beating well after each addition. Add flavouring. Beat until smooth.

Add next 4 ingredients. Beat well.

Combine flour, baking powder and baking soda in small bowl. Add to margarine mixture. Mix until no dry flour remains.

Combine next 6 ingredients in same small bowl. Add to batter. Mix well. Grease 12 muffin cups with cooking spray. Fill cups 3/4 full. Bake in 325°F (160°C) oven for 20 to 25 minutes until wooden pick inserted in centre of fruitcake comes out clean. Let stand in pan for 10 minutes before removing to wire rack set on baking sheet to cool.

Randomly poke several holes with skewer in top of each fruitcake. Drizzle 1/2 tsp. (2 mL) second amount of rum over each. Turn fruitcakes over. Randomly poke several holes with skewer in bottom of each fruitcake. Drizzle 1/2 tsp. (2 mL) rum over each.

Place cheesecloth squares in small bowl. Pour third amount of rum over top. Let stand until rum is absorbed, adding more rum if necessary to soak cheesecloth. Wrap each fruitcake with 1 cheesecloth square. Wrap each with waxed paper. Wrap each tightly with foil. Store in refrigerator for 2 weeks. Check fruitcakes after 1 week. Moisten cheesecloths with additional rum if necessary. Unwrap fruitcakes. Place on cake plate.

Coconut Glaze: Stir icing sugar, pineapple juice and flavouring in small bowl, adding more icing sugar or pineapple juice if necessary, until barely pourable consistency. Makes about 2 tbsp. (30 mL) glaze. Spoon into piping bag fitted with small writing tip or into small resealable freezer bag with tiny piece snipped off corner. Drizzle glaze in decorative pattern over each fruitcake. Let stand until set. Makes 12 fruitcakes.

1 fruitcake: 371 Calories; 14.8 g Total Fat (8.1 g Mono, 1.8 g Poly, 3.9 g Sat); 36 mg Cholesterol; 51 g Carbohydrate; 2 g Fibre; 4 g Protein; 161 mg Sodium

Pictured on page 159 and on page 183.

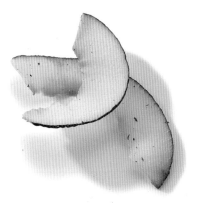

Top Left and Bottom: Tropical Fruitcakes, this page
Right: Hawaiian Shortbread Squares, page 156

Wrapping It Up

You've created some wonderful gifts for everyone on your list, now all that's left is to dazzle them with your own custom wrapping. No matter what your style or ability, you can easily create attractive gift bags, boxes and wrapping paper and add some special little touches to make holiday gift giving fun.

Easy-to-follow instructions and colourful pictures show you how simple it can be. Collect items throughout the year that might make a clever adornment, or look to page 9 for some helpful ideas for things to have on hand. Draw inspiration from our suggestions or from any of the ideas pictured throughout the book. Then be bold with your imagination, add a personal touch and wrap your gift in your own unique style. Remember that gift giving is a year-long event and many of these suggestions can easily be adapted to suit other special occasions.

Gifting With Bags

Paper bags can be adorned in many creative ways as shown in the picture on page 161. All it takes is a little imagination, fabric and ribbon remnants, bows, assorted Christmas embellishments and some glue.

Fabric Appliqué Gift Bag

MATERIALS

Fabric with large Christmas motif
Iron-on adhesive
Brown paper bag (4 3/4 x 8 1/2 inches, 12 x 21 cm)
Coloured buttons
Natural raffia

TOOLS

scissors, iron, fine black marker, white craft glue, hole punch

Cut around the motif on the fabric, leaving about a 1/2 inch (1.2 cm) border. Iron the adhesive according to the package directions onto the wrong side of the motif. Carefully trim the border from the motif. Remove the paper backing and iron the motif onto the bag.

Draw stitching lines on the bag around the motif. Glue on some buttons to decorate. Fill the bag with your homemade gift. Fold the top down. Punch 2 holes 1/2 inch (1.2 cm) apart. Thread raffia through the holes and tie a bow.

Pictured on page 161.

Away In A Manger Gift Bag

MATERIALS

Felt pieces (9 x 12 inches, 22 x 30 cm, each), yellow, blue, burgundy, brown, champagne
Brown chenille stem
Brown paper bag (4 3/4 x 8 1/2 inches, 12 x 21 cm)

TOOLS

scissors, pins, white craft glue, wire cutters

Enlarge the pattern to 125% (this page). Cut out each piece. Pin the enlarged pattern pieces to the felt colours as follows:

Yellow: Cut out 1 star. Cut thin strip for straw and pull apart to make about 8 small pieces.

Blue: Cut out the figure of Joseph.

Burgundy: Cut out the figure of Mary.

Brown: Cut out the cradle and Joseph's headband.

Champagne: Cut out baby Jesus' head and 2 hands.

Use the picture as a guide to assemble the felt pieces. Glue the headband onto Joseph. Glue along the flat edge of 1 hand and attach the edge behind his body. Glue Jesus' head behind the cradle so that half of the head is visible. Glue the straw onto the top of the cradle. Glue along the flat edge of the remaining hand and attach the edge behind Mary's body so that the hand is in a praying position. Shape the chenille stem to make Joseph's staff. Trim to fit. Lay the bag flat. Glue on the felt pieces and chenille staff according to the picture on page 161. Let dry completely. Fill the bag with your homemade gift.

Pictured on page 161.

Pattern pieces for Away In A Manger Gift Bag

Photo legend, previous page
Top Left: Away In A Manger Gift Bag, this page
Top Centre: Window Gift Bag, page 163
Top Right: Fabric Appliqué Gift Bag, this page
Bottom Left: Woven Ribbon Gift Bag, page 163

Wrapping It Up ✶ *162*

Window Gift Bag

MATERIALS
Cardboard piece (5 x 8 inches, 12.5 x 20 cm)
Coloured paper bag (5 1/4 x 10 inches, 13 x 25 cm)
Christmas tree cookie cutter
White chenille stem
Overhead transparency sheet
Felt star (1 inch, 2.5 cm, diameter)
3 coloured buttons
Ribbon (1/4 inch, 6 mm, width), 12 inch (30 cm) length

TOOLS
pencil, Exacto knife, pinking shears, wire cutters, scissors, tape, glue gun, hole punch

Place the cardboard piece inside the bag as a cutting surface. Centre the cookie cutter 1 inch (2.5 cm) from the bottom of the bag. Trace around the cookie cutter. Cut out the tree shape with the Exacto knife.

Trim the top of the bag with pinking shears. Fold the chenille stem in half to find the centre. Place the centre of the stem at the top of the cut-out and bend each side to follow the tree shape. With wire cutters, cut off any excess stem. Cut a rectangle from the transparency sheet a bit larger than the cut-out. Remove the cardboard from the bag and insert the rectangle behind the cut-out. Tape it into place on the inside of the bag. Working on the outside of the bag, glue around the edge of the cut-out so the glue makes contact with the bag and the transparency sheet. Working quickly, press the shaped chenille stem onto the glued area. Glue the star and the buttons onto the cut-out. Let dry completely. Fill the bag with your homemade gift. Fold the top down. Punch 2 holes 1/2 inch (1.2 cm) apart. Thread ribbon through the holes and tie a bow.

Pictured on page 114 and on page 161.

Woven Ribbon Gift Bag

MATERIALS
Coloured paper bag (5 1/4 x 10 inches, 13 x 25 cm)
Cardboard piece (5 x 8 inches, 12.5 x 20 cm)
Ribbon (1 inch, 2.5 cm, width), 24 inch (60 cm) length

TOOLS
pinking shears, ruler, pencil, Exacto knife, scissors, white craft glue, tape

Trim 2 inches (5 cm) from the top of the bag with pinking shears. Lay the ruler along the top of the bag. Starting from 1 side, make 4 marks at 1 inch (2.5 cm) intervals. Repeat at the bottom of the bag, starting from the same side. Lay the ruler along the side of the bag, aligning at the top and bottom with the first of the 1 inch (2.5 cm) markings. Starting at the bottom of the bag, draw four 1 inch (2.5 cm) vertical lines at 3/4, 2 3/4, 4 3/4 and 6 3/4 inches (2, 7, 12 and 17 cm). Repeat, aligning the ruler at each of the remaining marked measurements at the top and bottom of the bag. You should finish with 4 rows of four 1 inch (2.5 cm) lines. Place the cardboard inside the bag as a cutting surface. Carefully cut each line with the Exacto knife. Remove the cardboard.

Cut four 5 1/4 inch (13.5 cm) lengths of ribbon. Put your hand inside the bag to help weave. Start at the bottom, from the outside of the bag. Weave the ribbon down into the first slot, and up through the next slot, repeating to the end of the row. To secure the ribbon, centre and glue both ends onto the outside of the bag. On the next row, start weaving from the inside of the bag. To secure the ribbon, centre and tape both ends onto the inside of the bag. Repeat with the remaining 2 rows. Fill the bag with your homemade gift.

Pictured on page 161.

Photo legend, next page
Top Right: Denim-Wrapped Box, page 166
Centre Right: Vegetable-Stamped Paper, page 166
Bottom Right: Mulberry Box, page 166

Made especially
for you by
Recipe

Gift Wrapping

Homemade gift wrapping is limited only by imagination. Fabric, doilies, decorative paper, ribbon and an assortment of embellishments and decorations, in various combinations, add a unique, personal touch to any gift. We hope you'll be inspired by the crafts on these pages and the other ideas pictured on page 164.

Denim-Wrapped Box

MATERIALS
Square box (about 10 inches, 60 cm)
Denim fabric (1/2 yd., 1/2 m)
Embellishments (such as beads, sequins or rivets)

TOOLS
ruler, scissors, pencil, glue gun, light-coloured fabric pen

Add together the height of 2 sides and the width of the bottom of the box, plus 1 inch (2.5 cm). Cut out a square of denim the size of this measurement. Centre the box on the wrong side of the denim square. With a pencil, mark the corners of the box onto the denim. Remove the box.

Draw a straight line from each marked corner to the edge of the denim (see picture). Cut the fabric along the lines.

Place the bottom of the box on the denim, aligning it with the marked corners. Pull up 1 long side of the denim and fold the ends around the corners of the box (see picture). Glue in place. Fold the excess fabric over the rim of the box and glue it to the inside. Repeat with the opposite long side. Pull up each short side, folding the excess denim over the rim of the box. Glue in place.

Measure the box lid in the same way, cut out a second denim square, and wrap in the same way.

Cut out a pocket from the denim. On the wrong side, glue all but the top edge of the pocket. Centre it on the lid. Glue embellishments around the edges of the pocket. With a fabric pen, draw stitching lines on the pocket.

Pictured on page 165 and page 176.

Mulberry Box

MATERIALS
Sheet of red mulberry paper (see Note)
Sheet of gold mulberry paper
Glossy decoupage paste (such as Mod Podge)
Medium-size papier mâché box

TOOLS
sponge brush

Tear both sheets of mulberry paper into small pieces. Brush some decoupage paste onto a small section of the box. Place some of the paper pieces on top of the paste, overlapping to cover the area, and alternating colours as desired. Fold the excess paper over the rim of the box and paste to the inside. Brush some paste on top of the paper pieces. Repeat, overlapping the paper until the entire box is covered. Cover the lid in the same way, beginning on the sides. Let dry completely.

Pictured on page 165.

Note: Packages of mulberry paper are available at craft supply stores.

Vegetable-Stamped Paper

MATERIALS
Potato (or other vegetable or fruit)
Acrylic paint
Plain paper

TOOLS
pencil, Exacto knife, foam brush

Cut potato in half. With a pencil, draw a simple design on the cut-side of the potato. With the Exacto knife, score the potato along the pencilled design, cutting about 1/4 inch (6 mm) deep.

Carefully cut away the excess potato to the edge of the design, 1/4 inch (6 mm) from the top. Pour some paint into a shallow dish. Paint the potato stamp with a foam brush. Press the stamp onto the paper, repainting as necessary.

Pictured on page 165.

Top: Natural Greenery Bow, page 168
Bottom Right: Jingle Bell Wreath, page 168
Bottom Left: Ribbon Rose Bow, page 169

Gift Adornments

*Adorn your gifts with one of these seasonal crafts.
Beads, berries, bows, greenery and pinecones—the options
are limitless—make homemade gift giving especially fun.
Like the icing on a cake, the ideas on these pages and those
pictured on page 167 will add the perfect finishing touch.*

Natural Greenery Bow

MATERIALS
Fresh cedar boughs
Cardboard circle (3 inch, 7.5 cm, diameter)
**Mulberry paper ribbon (1 1/2 inch, 3.8 cm, width),
    3 yd. (2.75 m) length**
Florist wire (32 gauge), or twist tie
Natural raffia
Miscellaneous twigs, berries and pine cones

TOOLS
glue gun, scissors, wire cutters

Glue the stem-ends of 2 small cedar bough branches onto the centre of the cardboard circle so the greenery extends outward. (The cardboard base allows the recipient to easily remove the bow from the package.)

Hold the ribbon between your thumb and forefinger, about 3 inches (7.5 cm) from 1 end. Form a 6 inch (15 cm) loop and pinch it between your thumb and forefinger to hold in place. Twist the ribbon at the pinch. Form a second loop, making the other side of the bow. Pinch to hold in place, then twist the ribbon at the pinch.

Continue looping, pinching and twisting at the centre, alternating sides, until desired fullness. Wrap the florist wire around the centre of the loops and tightly twist-tie at the back. Trim the ends of the wire. Glue the bow onto the centre of the cedar boughs. Spread and fluff the loops.

Repeat the bow technique with the raffia, tying the centre tightly with a strand of raffia. Glue onto the centre of the ribbon bow. Spread the raffia loops through the ribbon loops. Glue and tuck a few pieces of cedar into the centre of the bow. Glue twigs, berries and pine cones onto the cedar boughs as desired. Glue the arrangement to the gift.

Pictured on page 155 and on page 167.

Jingle Bell Wreath

MATERIALS
**Package of multi-coloured jingle bells (1/2 inch,
    12 mm, diameter)**
Glittered chenille stem

Alternating colours, slide the bells onto the chenille stem, leaving 2 inches (5 cm) of stem uncovered at each end. Twist the stem ends together to secure the bells. Curl the ends. Use as a unique bow or to decorate a bottle.

Pictured on page 160 and on page 167.

Ribbon Roses

MATERIALS
Florist ribbon #9 (1 3/8 inch, 3.4 cm, width)
Green florist tape
Florist wire (22 gauge)
Small craft leaves (optional)

TOOLS
ruler, scissors, wire cutters

Fold the ribbon according to the diagram to make a 1 1/2 inch (3.8 cm) tail, keeping the ribbon roll to your right.

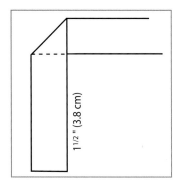

To make the centre of the rose, roll the ribbon to the right from point A to point B.

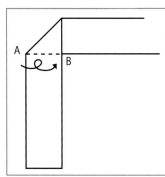

Place the thumb of your right hand behind the ribbon on the right. Twist the ribbon away from you to make a triangle (point C on the diagram). Roll the centre of the rose twice to the right, toward the point of the triangle.

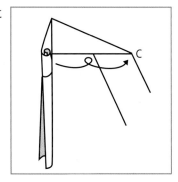

Twist the ribbon to make another triangle. To make a petal, roll the centre of the rose just once, to the right toward point C on the diagram. Repeat, to make the ribbon rose as big as you like, making sure the petals stay above the centre of the rose.

To finish the rose, twist the ribbon to make a final triangle. Bring the ribbon downward to form another tail. Pinch the bottom of the rose. At the pinch, twist the tails tightly twice. Hold securely and trim both tails to 1 inch (2.5 cm). Wrap florist tape tightly around the bottom of the rose where the tails are twisted to form the base. Attach the florist wire to the base with florist tape, wrapping from the bottom of the rose downward onto the wire until the desired stem length is covered. Trim the tape and any unwrapped wire. Glue leaves onto the stem and base of the rose.

Pictured on page 167.

Ribbon Rose Bow

MATERIALS
3 Ribbon Roses, this page
Cardboard circle (1 1/2 inch, 3.8 cm, diameter)
3 small craft leaves
3 craft pearl strands (2 inch, 5 cm, length, each)
3 tulle circles (1 inch, 2.5 cm, diameter, each)

TOOLS
wire cutters, glue gun

Trim the stems of the ribbon roses to 1/4 inch (6 mm). Glue the roses to the cardboard circle, stems toward the centre and roses just touching. Glue the leaves between the roses. Loop the pearl strands, glue the ends, and place between the leaves and roses. Pinch the centres of the tulle circles, glue at the pinch, and place between the roses. Glue the cardboard base to your wrapped gift.

Pictured on page 167.

Tag - A - Longs

Need a cute and unique idea for labelling your gifts?
Try one of these. More ideas are pictured on the right.

Cookie Cutter Tag

MATERIALS
Christmas cookie cutter
Peel-and-stick felt piece
Craft pearl or bead strand
Fabric paint

TOOLS
pencil, scissors

Trace the cookie cutter shape onto the felt. Cut out the shape.
Thread the pearl strand through the cookie cutter. With fabric
paint, write your message on the felt. Let dry completely. Peel
off the backing of the felt. Stick the felt onto the cookie cutter,
aligning them together. Attach the pearl strand to your gift.
Great to use when giving cut-out cookies.

Gingerbread People Tags

MATERIALS
Gingerbread Cookies, page 68, cut out into gingerbread
   people
Quick And Easy Royal Icing, page 66
Chenille stems

Before baking the cookies, make a hole in each, 1/4 inch
(6 mm) from the top of the head. After baking, decorate
the cookies and write your messages with icing. Let dry
completely. Thread the chenille stems through the holes
and attach to your gifts.

Clear Ball Ornament

MATERIALS
Clear plastic ball that can be opened (3 inch,
   7.5 cm, diameter)
Small coloured candies
Fabric paint
Ribbon

Fill both halves of the ball with candies. Close the ball. With
fabric paint, write your message on the ball. Let dry
completely. Attach to your gift with ribbon.

Top Left: Cookie Cutter Tag, this page
Bottom Right: Gingerbread People Tags, this page
Bottom Centre: Clear Ball Ornament, above

Themed Gift Baskets

Try one of these creative ways to package an assortment of recipes from this book to give to a deserving someone.

Ice Cream Sundae

Have an ice cream lover on your list? Fill a festive basket or box with these delectable sauces. Wrap a stack of edible Cookie Sundae Bowls with cellophane and tuck them in the basket. Include an ice cream scoop, some spoons tied together with ribbon, and a shaker brimming with colourful candy sprinkles.

Pictured on pages 172/173.

Kid's Best Friend

What a great way to say "I'm glad we're friends!" Fill the Snowman Jar with Snowman-In-A-Mug Mix and put it in a cheerful basket along with these sweet treats and the recipe for making the pizza. Complete your gift with a colourful Christmas mug, a stuffed animal and an activity book. When the drink mix is all gone, the Snowman Jar makes a great keepsake, too.

Pictured on page 174.

Chocolate Lover's

Chocolate is such a sweet, alluring treat. Wrap up this selection of everything chocolate in decorative cellophane, bottles and jars, and embellish the containers with a little help from our Gift Adornment and Tag-A-Long ideas, pages 168 to 171. Put it all in a seasonal basket and add a holiday mug.

Pictured on page 175.

Photo legend, next page
Left: Kid's Best Friend, this page
Right: Chocolate Lover's, above

College Care Package

Send your college student back to the books with this thoughtful care package. Wrap a jar of Calico Bean Soup Mix in a Christmas tea towel and put it in a Denim-Wrapped Box or in a handy new book bag. Include the recipe for turning the Biscuit Mix into hot, steaming treats to top with Two Berry Jam—a comforting snack when thoughts turn to home. Finish the basket with a bag of Oriental Crunch to ward off the late night munchies.

Pictured above.

Snack Attack

Pita Scoops	page 106
Nacho Shake	page 57
Parmesan Dill Shake	page 57
Tapenade Salsa	page 82
G-Rated Punch Mix	page 41

Great for movie night at home. A basket or bowl filled with these savoury snacks wrapped in decorative cellophane, shakers and jars is sure to entice. Pair the G-Rated Punch Mix with a set of colourful drinking glasses. Include a package of unpopped popcorn and a favourite video, and let the show begin!

Pictured above.

Stress Buster

When a friend or family member is feeling the stress of the season, pamper them with this lovely assortment of treats. Package the Pink Chocolate Truffles in a pretty box and put it in a beautiful basket. Lavender Milk Bath Bags and an attractive bottle of Lavender Massage Oil will nestle nicely in this inviting collection. Relaxation is guaranteed with a glass of wine made with the mulling kit. Complete this gift with a selection of soothing music, scented candles and a soft, new bath towel.

Pictured on page 178.

Tea Break

What a "tea-rrific" gift for the tea lover you know. Pair a decorative jar of soothing Tummy Tea Mix with a cheerful teacup, and put them in a basket or bowl. Sweet tea time treats and a scented trivet are sensational additions. Be sure to include the recipe for making the muffins. Tuck a journal and pen in the basket for recording personal reflections while taking a much-deserved break.

Pictured on pages 178/179.

Left: Stress Buster, this page
Right: Tea Break, above

Barbecue Basket

Barbecue Seasoning	page 56
Teriyaki Marinade	page 80
Rosemary Lemon Rub	page 56
Zucchini Relish	page 86

Grilling has become a year-round activity enjoyed by men and women alike. Cooks will love this selection of barbecue essentials presented in a new grilling basket. Be sure to include the recipe suggestions for using the seasonings. Add a fun apron, oven mitts for the grill, a barbecue cookbook and some shiny new utensils. And don't forget the napkins!

Pictured above.

Mexican Basket

Tijuana Triangles	page 106
Roma Lime Salsa	page 82
Fiesta Relish	page 85

This spicy gift makes any time fiesta time! Tijuana Triangles are perfect for dipping in Roma Lime Salsa and Fiesta Relish. Arrange these tasty snacks in a colourful basket or box, and add a package of brightly coloured napkins and a chip-and-dip serving dish. Complete your gift with a Mexican cookbook. Olé!

Pictured on page 181.

Italian Basket

Invite your friends and family to enjoy a taste of Italy with this savoury collection. Wrap it up in a colourful basket or bowl with a bottle of olive oil, a package of colourful dried pasta and a wedge of fresh Parmesan cheese. A bottle of red wine, a checkered cloth and an Italian cookbook add the perfect touch.

Pictured above.

Sun-Seeker's Basket

Know anyone who's heading south for the winter, or wishes they were? Create a warming gift basket with these tropical treats and a CD of Latin music for some sizzling hot fun! For a touch of whimsy, decorate your gift with seashells and paper umbrellas.

Pictured on page 183.

Good Neighbour Gift

Amaretto Mochaccino Mix page 46
Pecan Truffles page 142
Cashew Buttercrunch page 120

Give your special neighbours a basket of homemade goodies to thank them for all the thoughtful things they do. Warm them, body and soul, with Amaretto Mochaccino Mix, and sooth their sweet tooth with Pecan Truffles and Cashew Buttercrunch. Complete your gift with holiday mugs and napkins, and your neighbours will be thanking you!

Pictured above.

Measurement Tables

Throughout this book measurements are given in Conventional and Metric measure. To compensate for differences between the two measurements due to rounding, a full metric measure is not always used. The cup used is the standard 8 fluid ounce. Temperature is given in degrees Fahrenheit and Celsius. Baking pan measurements are in inches and centimetres as well as quarts and litres. An exact metric conversion is given on this page as well as the working equivalent (Standard Measure).

Oven Temperatures

Fahrenheit (°F)	Celsius (°C)	Fahrenheit (°F)	Celsius (°C)
175°	80°	350°	175°
200°	95°	375°	190°
225°	110°	400°	205°
250°	120°	425°	220°
275°	140°	450°	230°
300°	150°	475°	240°
325°	160°	500°	260°

Spoons

Conventional Measure	Metric Exact Conversion Millilitre (mL)	Metric Standard Measure Millilitre (mL)
1/8 teaspoon (tsp.)	0.6 mL	0.5 mL
1/4 teaspoon (tsp.)	1.2 mL	1 mL
1/2 teaspoon (tsp.)	2.4 mL	2 mL
1 teaspoon (tsp.)	4.7 mL	5 mL
2 teaspoons (tsp.)	9.4 mL	10 mL
1 tablespoon (tbsp.)	14.2 mL	15 mL

Cups

1/4 cup (4 tbsp.)	56.8 mL	60 mL
1/3 cup (5 1/3 tbsp.)	75.6 mL	75 mL
1/2 cup (8 tbsp.)	113.7 mL	125 mL
2/3 cup (10 2/3 tbsp.)	151.2 mL	150 mL
3/4 cup (12 tbsp.)	170.5 mL	175 mL
1 cup (16 tbsp.)	227.3 mL	250 mL
4 1/2 cups	1022.9 mL	1000 mL (1 L)

Pans

Conventional Inches	Metric Centimetres
8 × 8 inch	20 × 20 cm
9 × 9 inch	22 × 22 cm
9 × 13 inch	22 × 33 cm
10 × 15 inch	25 × 38 cm
11 × 17 inch	28 × 43 cm
8 × 2 inch round	20 × 5 cm
9 × 2 inch round	22 × 5 cm
10 × 4 1/2 inch tube	25 × 11 cm
8 × 4 × 3 inch loaf	20 × 10 × 7.5 cm
9 × 5 × 3 inch loaf	22 × 12.5 × 7.5 cm

Dry Measurements

Conventional Measure Ounces (oz.)	Metric Exact Conversion Grams (g)	Metric Standard Measure Grams (g)
1 oz.	28.3 g	28 g
2 oz.	56.7 g	57 g
3 oz.	85.0 g	85 g
4 oz.	113.4 g	125 g
5 oz.	141.7 g	140 g
6 oz.	170.1 g	170 g
7 oz.	198.4 g	200 g
8 oz.	226.8 g	250 g
16 oz.	453.6 g	500 g
32 oz.	907.2 g	1000 g (1 kg)

Casseroles

Canada & Britain

Standard Size Casserole	Exact Metric Measure
1 qt. (5 cups)	1.13 L
1 1/2 qts. (7 1/2 cups)	1.69 L
2 qts. (10 cups)	2.25 L
2 1/2 qts. (12 1/2 cups)	2.81 L
3 qts. (15 cups)	3.38 L
4 qts. (20 cups)	4.5 L
5 qts. (25 cups)	5.63 L

United States

Standard Size Casserole	Exact Metric Measure
1 qt. (4 cups)	900 mL
1 1/2 qts. (6 cups)	1.35 L
2 qts. (8 cups)	1.8 L
2 1/2 qts. (10 cups)	2.25 L
3 qts. (12 cups)	2.7 L
4 qts. (16 cups)	3.6 L
5 qts. (20 cups)	4.5 L

Craft & Gifting Index